THE ROSICRUCIAN MYSTERIES AN ELEMENTARY EXPOSITION OF THEIR SECRET TEACHINGS • HEINDEL, MAX

Chapter I. The Order of Rosicrucians and the Rosicrucian Fellowship 1
Chapter II. The Problem of Life and Its Solution 4
Chapter III. The Visible and the Invisible World 9
Chapter IV. The Constitution of Man 21
Chapter V. Life and Death 24
Mt. Ecclesia 36
Index 38

Publisher's Note

Purchase of this book entitles you to a free trial membership in the publisher's book club at www.rarebooksclub.com. (Time limited offer.) Simply enter the barcode number from the back cover onto the membership form on our home page. The book club entitles you to select from millions of books at no additional charge. You can also download a digital copy of this and related books to read on the go. Simply enter the title or subject onto the search form to find them.

Note: This is an historic book. Pages numbers, where present in the text, refer to the first edition of the book and may also be in indexes.

If you have any questions, could you please be so kind as to consult our Frequently Asked Questions page at www.rarebooksclub.com/faqs.cfm? You are also welcome to contact us there.
Publisher: General Books LLC™, Memphis, TN, USA, 2012. ISBN: 9781153822206.
Proofreading: pgdp.net

❧ ❧ ❧ ❧ ❧ ❧ ❧ ❧

The
   Rosicrucian Mysteries
   An Elementary Exposition of
   Their Secret Teachings
   By
   Max Heindel
   Author of: The Rosicrucian Cosmo Conception, The Rosicrucian Philosophy in Questions and Answers, The Rosicrucian Interpretation of Christianity, Rays from the Rose Cross, etc.
   Third Edition
   Rosicrucian Fellowship
   Oceanside, California
   London
   L. N. Fowler, 7 Imperial Arcade
   Ludgate Circus. E. C.

[pg 005]

Chapter I. The Order of Rosicrucians and the Rosicrucian Fellowship

Our Message And Mission
   A Sane Mind
   A Soft Heart
   A Sound Body

Before entering upon an explanation of the teachings of the Rosicrucians, it may be well to say a word about them and about the place they hold in the evolution of humanity.

For reasons to be given later these teachings advocate the dualistic view; they hold that man is a spirit enfolding all the powers of God as the seed enfolds the plant, and that these powers are being slowly unfolded by a series of existences in a gradually improving earthy body; also that this process of development has been performed under the guidance of exalted beings who are yet ordering our steps, though in a decreasing [pg 006] measure, as we gradually acquire intellect and will. These exalted Beings, though unseen to the physical eyes, are nevertheless potent factors in all affairs of life, and give to the various groups of humanity lessons which will most efficiently promote the growth of their spiritual powers. In fact, the earth may be likened to a vast training school in which there are pupils of varying age and ability as we find it in one of our own schools. There are the savages, living and worshipping under most primitive conditions, seeing in stick or stone a God. Then, as man progresses onwards and upwards in the scale of civilization, we find a higher and higher conception of Deity, which has flowered here in our Western World in the beautiful Christian religion that now furnishes our spiritual inspiration and incentive to improve.

These various religions have been given to each group of humanity by the exalted beings whom we know in the Christian religion as the Recording Angels, whose wonderful prevision enable them to view the trend of even so unstable a quantity as the human mind, and thus they are enabled to determine what steps are necessary to lead [pg 007] our enfoldment along the lines congruous to the highest universal good.

When we study the history of the ancient nations we shall find that at about six hundred years B. C. a great spiritual wave had its inception on the Eastern shores of the Pacific Ocean where the great Confucian Religion accelerated the progress of the Chinese nation, then also the Religion of the Buddha commenced to win its millions of adherents in India, and still further West we have the lofty philosophy of Pythagoras. Each system was suited to the needs of the particular people to whom it was sent. Then came the period of the Sceptics, in Greece, and later, traveling westward the same spiritual wave is manifested as the Christian religion of the so-called "Dark Ages" when the dogma of a dominant church compelled belief from the whole of Western Europe.

It is a law in the universe that a wave of spiritual awakening is always followed by a period of doubting materialism, each phase is necessary in order that the spirit may receive equal development of heart and intellect without being carried too far in either direction.

The Great Beings aforementioned, Who care for our progress, always [pg 008] take steps to safeguard humanity against that danger, and when they foresaw the wave of materialism which commenced in the sixteenth century with the birth of our modern Science, they took steps to protect the West as they had formerly safeguarded the East against the Sceptics who were held in check by the Mystery schools.

In the thirteenth century there appeared in central Europe a great spiritual teacher whose symbolical name was

Christian Rosenkreuz.

or

Christian Rose Cross.

who founded the mysterious Order of the Rosy Cross, concerning which so many speculations have been made and so little has become known to the world at large, for it is the Mystery school of the West and is only open to those who have attained the stage of spiritual unfoldment necessary to be initiated in its secrets concerning the Science of Life and Being.

If we are so far developed that we are able to leave our dense physical body and take a soul flight into interplanetary space we shall find that the ultimate physical atom [pg 009] is spherical in shape like our earth; it is a ball. When we take a number of balls of even size and group them around one, it will take just twelve balls to hide a thirteenth within. Thus the twelve visible and the one hidden are numbers revealing a cosmic relationship and as all Mystery Orders are based upon cosmic lines, they are composed of twelve members gathered around a thirteenth who is the invisible *head*.

There are seven colors in the spectrum: red, orange, yellow, green, blue, indigo and violet. But between the violet and the red there are still other five colors which are invisible to the physical eye but reveal themselves to the spiritual sight. In every Mystery Order there are also seven brothers who at times go out into the world and there perform whatever work may be necessary to advance the people among whom they serve, but five are never seen outside the temple. They work with and teach those alone who have passed through certain stages of spiritual unfoldment and are able to visit the temple in their spiritual bodies; a feat taught in the first initiation which usually takes place outside the temple as it is not [pg 010] convenient for all to visit that place physically.

Let not the reader imagine that this initiation makes the pupil a Rosicrucian, it does not, any more than admission to a High School makes a boy a member of the faculty. Nor does he become a Rosicrucian even after having passed through all the nine degrees of this or any other Mystery School. The Rosicrucians are Hierophants of the lesser Mysteries, and beyond them there are still schools wherein Greater Mysteries are taught. Those who have advanced through the lesser Mysteries and have become pupils of the Greater Mysteries are called Adepts, but even they have not reached the exalted standpoint of the twelve Brothers of the Rosicrucian Order or the Hierophants of any other lesser Mystery School any more than the freshman at college has attained to the knowledge and position of a teacher in the High school from which he has just graduated.

A later work will deal with initiation, but we may say here that the door of a genuine Mystery School is not unlocked by a golden key, but is only opened as a reward for meritorious service to humanity and any one [pg 011] who advertises himself as a Rosicrucian or makes a charge for tuition, by either of those acts shows himself to be a charlatan. The true pupil of any Mystery School is far too modest to advertise the fact, he will scorn all titles or honors from men, he will have no regard for riches save the riches of love given to him by those whom it becomes his privilege to help and teach.

In the centuries that have gone by since the Rosicrucian Order was first formed they have worked quietly and secretly, aiming to mould the thought of Western Europe through the works of Paracelsus, Boehme, Bacon, Shakespeare, Fludd and others. Each night at midnight when the physical activities of the day are at their lowest ebb, and the spiritual impulse at its highest flood tide, they have sent out from their temple soul-stirring vibrations to counteract materialism and to further the development of soul powers. To their activities we owe the gradual spiritualization of our once so materialistic science.

With the commencement of the twentieth century a further step was taken. It was realized that something must be done to make [pg 012] religion scientific as well as to make science religious, in order that they may ultimately blend; for at the present time heart and intellect are divorced. The heart instinctively feels the truth of religious teachings concerning such wonderful mysteries as the Immaculate Conception (the Mystic Birth), the Crucifixion (the Mystic Death), the cleansing blood, the atonement, and other doctrines of the Church, which the intellect refuses to believe, as they are incapable of demonstration, and seemingly at war with natural law. Material advancement may be furthered when intellect is dominant and the longings of the heart unsatisfied, but soul growth will be retarded until the heart also receives satisfaction.

In order to give the world a teaching so blended that it will satisfy both the mind and heart, a messenger must be found and instructed. Certain unusual qualifications were necessary, and the first one chosen failed to pass a certain test after several years had been spent to prepare him for the work to be done.

It is well said that there is a time to sow, and a time to reap, and that there are certain times for all the works of life, and in accordance [pg 013] with this law of periodicity each impulse in spiritual uplift must also be undertaken at an appropriate time to be successful. The first and sixth decades of each century are particularly propitious to commence the promulgation of new spiritual teachings. Therefore the Rosicrucians were much concerned at this failure, for only five years were left of the first decade of the twentieth century.

Their second choice of a messenger fell upon the present writer, though he knew it not at the time, and by shaping circumstances about him they made it possible for him to begin a period of preparation for the work they desired him to do. Three years later, when he had gone to Germany, also because of circumstances shaped by the invisible Brotherhood, and was on the verge of despair at the discovery that the light which was the object of his quest, was only a jack-o-lantern, the Brothers of the Rosicrucian Order applied the test to see whether he would be a faithful messenger and give the teachings they desired to entrust to him, to the world. And when he had passed the trial they gave him the monumental solution of the problem of existence first published in "The Rosicrucian Cosmo Conception " in November, 1909, [pg 014] more than a year before the expiration of the first decade of the twentieth century. This book marked a new era in so-called "occult" literature, and the many editions which have since been published, as well as the thousands of letters which continue to come to the author, are speaking testimonies to the fact that people are finding in this teaching a satisfaction they have long sought elsewhere in vain.

The Rosicrucians teach that all great religions have been given to the people among whom they are found, by Divine Intelligences who designed each system of worship to suit the needs of the race or nation to whom it was given. A primitive people cannot respond to a lofty and sublime religion, and vice versa. What helps one race would hinder another, and in pursuance of the same policy there has been devised a system of soul-unfoldment suited specially to the Western people, who are racially and temperamentally unfit to undergo the discipline of the Eastern school, which was designed for the more backward Hindoos.

The Rosicrucian Fellowship

For the purpose of promulgating the Rosicrucian teachings in the Western World, the [pg 015] Rosicrucian Fellowship was founded in 1909. It is the herald of the Aquarian Age, when the Sun by its precessional passage through the constellation Aquarius will bring out all the intellectual and spiritual potencies in man which are symbolized by that sign. As heat from a fire warms all objects within the sphere of its radiations, so also the Aquarian ray will raise the earth's vibrations to a pitch we are as yet unable to comprehend, though we have demonstrations of the *material* workings of this force in the inventions which have revolutionized life within the memory of the present generation. We have wondered at the X-ray, which sees through the human body, but each one has a sense latent which when evolved will enable him to see through any number of bodies or to any distance. We marvel at the telephone conversations across the continent of America, but each has within a latent sense of speech and hearing that is far more acute; we are surprised at the exploits of ships under sea and in the sky, but we are all capable of passage under water or through the sky; nay, more, we may pass unscathed through the solid rock and the raging fire, if we know how, and lightning itself is slow compared to the speed with which we [pg 016] may travel. This sounds like a fairy tale today, as did Jules Verne's stories a generation ago, but the Aquarian Age will witness the realization of these dreams, and ever so much more that we still do not even dream of. Such faculties will then be the possessions of large numbers of people who will have gradually evolved them as previously the ability to walk, speak, hear, and see, were developed.

Therein lies a great danger, for, obviously, anyone endowed with such faculties may use them to the greatest detriment of the world at large, unless restrained by a spirit of unselfishness and an all-embracing altruism. Therefore religion is needed today as never before, to foster love and fellow-feeling among humanity so that it may be prepared to use the great gifts in store for it wisely and well. This need of religion is specially felt in a certain class where the ether is more loosely knit to the physical atoms than in the majority, and on that account they are now beginning to sense the Aquarian vibrations.

This class is again divided in two groups. In one the intellect is dominant, and the people in that class therefore seek to grasp the spiritual mysteries out of curiosity from the viewpoint of cold reason. They pursue the [pg 017] path of knowledge for the sake of knowledge, considering that an end in itself. The idea that knowledge is of value only when put to practical constructive use does not seem to have presented itself to them. This class we may call *occultists*.

The other group does not care for knowledge, but feels an inner urge Godward, and pursues the path of devotion to the high ideal set before them in Christ, doing the deeds that He did as far their flesh will permit, and this in time results in an interior illumination which brings with it all the knowledge obtained by the other class, and much more. This class we may describe as *mystics*.

Certain dangers confront each of the two groups. If the occultist obtains illumination and evolves within himself the latent spiritual faculties, he may use them for the furtherance of his personal objects, to the great detriment of his fellow-men. That is black magic, and the punishment which it *automatically* calls down upon the head of the perpetrator is so awful that it is best to draw the veil over it. The mystic may also err because of ignorance, and fall into the meshes of nature's law, but being actuated by love, his mistakes will never be very serious, and as he grows in grace the [pg 018] soundless voice within his heart will speak more distinctly to teach him the way.

The Rosicrucian Fellowship endeavors to prepare the world in general, and the sensitives of the two groups in particular, for the awakening of the latent powers in man, so that all may be guided safely through the danger-zone and be as well fitted as possible to use these new faculties. Effort is made to blend the love without which Paul declared a knowledge of all mysteries worthless, with a mystic knowledge rooted and grounded in love, so that the pupils of this school may become *living* exponents of this blended soul-science of the Western Wisdom School, and gradually educate humanity at large in the virtues necessary to make the possession of higher powers safe.

Note :—

Pages 19 to 26 inclusive, describing Mt. Ecclesia, have been transferred to the back of the book. (Transcriber's Note: They are pages 191 through 200 .)

[pg 027]

Chapter II. The Problem of Life and Its Solution

THE PROBLEM OF LIFE.

Among all the vicissitudes of life, which vary in each individual's experience, there is one event which sooner or later comes to everyone—Death! No matter what our station in life, whether the life lived has been a laudable one or the reverse, whether great achievements have marked our path among men, whether health or sickness have been our lot, whether we have been famous and surrounded by a host of admiring friends or have wandered unknown through the years of our life, at some time there comes a moment when we stand alone before the portal of death and are forced to take the leap into the dark.

The thought of this leap and of what lies beyond must inevitably force itself upon [pg 028] every thinking person. In the years of youth and health, when the bark of our life sails upon seas of prosperity, when all appears beautiful and bright, we may put the thought behind us, but there will surely come a time in the life of every thinking person when the problem of life and death forces itself upon his consciousness and refuses to be set aside. Neither will it help him to accept the ready made solution of anyone else without thought and in blind belief, for this is a basic problem which every one must solve for himself or herself in order to obtain satisfaction.

Upon the Eastern edge of the Desert of Sahara there stands the world-famous Sphinx with its inscrutable face turned toward the East, ever greeting the sun as its rising rays herald the newborn day. It was said in the Greek myth that it was the wont of this monster to ask a riddle of each traveler. She devoured those who could not answer, but when Oedipus solved the riddle she destroyed herself.

The riddle which she asked of men was the riddle of life and death, a query which is as relevant today as ever, and which each one must answer or be devoured in the jaws [pg 029] of death. But when once a person has found the solution to the problem, it will appear that in reality there is no death, that what appears so, is but a change from one state of *existence* to another. Thus, for the man who finds the true solution to the riddle of life, the sphinx of death has ceased to exist, and he can lift his voice in the triumphant cry "Oh death where is thy sting, oh grave where is thy victory."

Various theories of life have been advocated to solve this problem of life. We may divide them into two classes, namely *the monistic theory* , which holds that all the facts of life can be explained by reference to this visible world wherein we live, and *the dualistic theory* , which refers part of the phenomenon of life to another world which is now invisible to us.

Raphael in his famous painting "the School of Athens" has most aptly pictured to us the attitude of these two schools of thought. We see upon that marvelous painting a Greek Court such as those wherein philosophers were once wont to congregate. Upon the various steps which lead into the building a large number of men are engaged in deep conversation, but in the [pg 030] center at the top of the steps stand two figures, supposedly of Plato and Aristotle, one pointing upwards, the other towards the earth, each looking the other in the face, mutely, but with deeply concentrated will. Each seeking to convince the other that his attitude is right for each bears the conviction in his heart. One holds that he is of the earth earthy, that he has come from the dust and that thereto he will return, the other firmly advocates the position that there is a higher something which has always existed and will continue regardless of whether the body wherein it now dwells holds together or not.

The question who is right is still an open one with the majority of mankind. Millions of tons of paper and printer's ink have been used in futile attempts to settle it by argument, but it will always remain open to all who have not solved the riddle themselves, for it is a basic problem, a part of the life experience of every human being to settle that question, and therefore no one can give us the solution ready made for our acceptance. All that can be done by those who have really solved the problem, is to show to others the line along which they [pg 031] have found the solution, and thus direct the inquirer how he also may arrive at a conclusion.

That is the aim of this little book; not to offer a solution to the problem of life to be taken blindly, on faith in the author's ability of investigation. The teachings herein set forth are those handed down by the Great Western Mystery School of the Rosicrucian Order and are the result of the concurrent testimony of a long line of trained Seers given to the author and supplemented by his own independent investigation of the realms traversed by the spirit in its cyclic path from the invisible world to this plane of existence and back again.

Nevertheless, the student is warned that the writer may have misunderstood some of the teachings and that despite the greatest care he may have taken a wrong view of that which he believes to have seen in the invisible world where the possibilities of making a mistake are legion. Here in the world which we view about us the forms are stable and do not easily change, but in the world around us which is perceptible only by the spiritual sight, we may say that there is in reality no form, but that all is life. At least the [pg 032] forms are so changeable that the metamorphosis recounted in fairy stories is discounted there to an amazing degree, and therefore we have the surprising revelations of mediums and other untrained clairvoyants who, though they may be perfectly honest, are deceived by illusions of *form* which is evanescent, because they are incapable of viewing the *life* that is the permanent basis of that form.

We must learn to see in this world. The new-born babe has no conception of distance and will reach for things far, far beyond its grasp until it has learned to gauge its capacity. A blind man who acquires the faculty of sight, or has it restored by an operation, will at first be inclined to close his eyes when moving from place to place, and declare that it is easier to walk by feeling than by sight; that is because he has not learned to use his newly acquired faculty. Similarly the man whose spiritual vision has been newly opened requires to be trained, in fact he is in much greater need thereof than the babe and the blind man already mentioned. Denied that training he would be like a new-born babe placed in a nursery where the walls are lined with mirrors of different [pg 033] convex and concave curvatures, which would distort its own shape and the forms of its attendants. If allowed to grow up in such surroundings and unable to see the real shapes of itself and its nurses it would naturally believe that it saw many different and distorted shapes where in reality the mirrors were responsible for the illusion. Were the persons concerned in such an experiment and the child taken out of the illusory surroundings, it would be incapable of recognizing them until the matter had been properly explained. There are similar dangers of illusion to those who have developed spiritual sight, until they have been trained to discount the refraction and to view the *life* which is permanent and stable, disregarding the *form* which is evanescent and changeable. The danger of getting things out of focus always remains however and is so subtle that the writer feels an imperative duty to warn his readers to take all statements concerning the unseen world with the proverbial grain of salt, for he has no intention to deceive. He is therefore inclined rather to magnify than to minimize his limitations and would advise the student to accept nothing from the author's pen [pg 034] without reasoning it out for himself. Thus, if he is deceived, he will be self-deceived and the author is blameless.

Three Theories of Life.

Only three noteworthy theories have been offered as solutions to the riddle of existence and in order that the reader may be able to make the important choice between them, we will state briefly what they are and give some of the arguments which lead us to advocate the doctrine of Rebirth as the method which favors soul-growth and the ultimate attainment of perfection, thus offering the best solution to the problem of life.

1) The Materialistic Theory teaches that life is but a short journey from the cradle to the grave, that there is no higher intelligence in the universe than man; that his mind is produced by certain correlations of matter and that therefore death, and dissolution of the body terminate existence.

There was a day when the arguments of Materialistic philosophers seemed convincing, but as science advances it discovers more and more that there is a spiritual side to the universe. That life and consciousness may exist without being able to give us a sign, has been amply proven in the cases [pg 035] where a person who was entranced and thought dead for days has suddenly awakened and told all that had taken place around the body. Such eminent scientists as Sir Oliver Lodge, Camille Flammarion, Lombroso and other men of highest intelligence and scientific training, have unequivocally stated as the result of their investigations, that the intelligence which we call man survives death of the body and lives on in our midst as independently of whether we see them or not as light and color exist all about the blind man regardless of the fact that he does not perceive them. These scientists have reached their conclusion after years of careful investigation. They have found that the so-called dead can, and under certain circumstances do, communicate with us in such a manner that mistake is out of the question. We maintain that their testimony is worth more than the argument of materialism to the contrary, for it is based upon years of careful investigation, it is in harmony with such well established laws as the law of conservation of matter and the law of conservation of energy. Mind is a form of energy, and immune from destruction as claimed by the materialist. Therefore we disbar the [pg 036] materialistic theory as unsound, because out of harmony with the laws of nature and with well established facts.

2) The Theory of Theology claims that just prior to each birth a soul is created by God and enters into the world where it lives for a time varying from a few minutes to a few score of years; that at the end of this short span of life it returns through the portal of death to the invisible beyond, where it remains forever in a condition of happiness or misery according to the deeds done in the body during the few years it lived here.

Plato insisted upon the necessity of a clear definition of terms as a basis of argument and we contend that that is as necessary in discussing the problem of life from the Bible point of view as in arguments from the platonic standpoint. According to the Bible man is a composite being consisting of body, soul and spirit. The two latter are usually taken to be synonymous, but we insist that they are not interchangeable and present the following to support our dictum.

All things are in a state of vibration. Vibrations from objects in our surroundings are constantly impinging upon us and carry [pg 037] to our senses a cognition of the external world. The vibrations in the ether act upon our eyes so that we see, and vibrations in the air transmit sounds to the ear.

We also breathe the ether which is charged with pictures of our surroundings and the sounds in our environment, so that by means of the breath we receive at each moment of our life, *internally* an accurate picture of our external surroundings.

That is a scientific proposition. Science does not explain what becomes of these vibrations however, but according to the Rosicrucian Mystery teaching they are transmitted to the blood, and then etched upon a little atom in the heart as automatically as a moving picture is imprinted upon the sensitized film, and a record of sounds is engraven upon the phonographic disc. This breath-record starts with the first breath of the newborn babe and ends only with the last gasp of the dying man, and "soul" is a product of the breath. Genesis also shows the connection between breath and soul in the words: "And the Lord God formed man of the dust of the ground, and breathed into his nostrils the breath of life; and man became a living soul" (The same word: nephesh, is [pg 038] translated breath and soul in the above quotation.)

In the post mortem existence the breath-record is disposed of. The good acts of life produce feelings of pleasure and the intensity of attraction incorporates them into the spirit as soul-power. *Thus the breath-records of our good acts are the soul which is saved*, for by the union with the spirit they become immortal. As they accumulate life after life, we become more soulful and they are thus also the basis of soulgrowth.

The record of our evil acts is also derived from our breath in the moments when they were committed. The pain and suffering they bring cause the spirit to expel the breath-record from its being in Purgatory. As that cannot exist independently of the life-giving spirit, the breath-record of our sins disintegrates upon expurgation, and thus we see that "the soul that sinneth, it shall die." The memory of the suffering incidental to expurgation however, remains with the spirit as *conscience*, to deter from repetition of the same evil in later lives.

Thus both our good and evil acts are recorded through the agency of the breath, which is therefore the basis of the soul, but [pg 039] while the breath-record of good acts amalgamates with the spirit and lives on forever as an immortal soul, the breath-record of evil deeds is disintegrated; it is the soul that sinneth and dies.

While the Bible teaches that immortality of the soul is conditional upon well-doing, it makes no distinction in respect of the spirit. The statement is clear and emphatic that when . "The silver cord be loosed . then shall the dust return to the earth as it was and the spirit shall return to God who gave it."

Thus the Bible teaches that the body is made of dust and returns thereto, that a part of the soul generated in the breath is perishable, but that the spirit survives bodily death and persists forever. Therefore a "lost soul" in the common acceptance of that term is not a Bible teaching, for the spirit is uncreate and eternal as God Himself, and therefore the orthodox theory cannot be true.

3) The Theory of Rebirths which teaches that each spirit is an integral part of God, that it enfolds all divine possibilities as the acorn enfolds the oak; that by means of many existences in an earthy body of gradually [pg 040] improving texture its latent powers are being slowly unfolded and become available as dynamic energy; that none can be lost but that all will ultimately attain to perfection and reunion with God, each bringing with it the accumulated experience which is the fruitage of its pilgrimage through matter.

Or, as we may poetically express it:
WE ARE ETERNAL.
On whistling stormcloud; on Zephyrus wing,
The Spirit-choir loud the World-anthems sing
Hark! Lis't to their voice " we have passed through death's door
There's no Death; rejoice! life lives evermore. "
We are, have always been, will ever be.
We are a portion of Eternity
Older than Creation, a part of One Great Whole,
Is each Individual and immortal Soul.
[pg 041]
On Time's whirring loom our garments we've wrought
Eternally weave we on network of Thought,
Our kin and our country, by Mind brought to birth,
Were patterned in heaven ere molded on earth.
We have shone in the Jewel and danced on the Wave,
We have sparkled in Fire defying the grave;
Through shapes everchanging, in size, kind and name
Our individual essence still is the same.
And when we have reached to the highest of all,
The gradations of growth our minds shall recall
So that link by link we may join them together
And trace step by step the way we reached thither.
Thus in time we shall know, if only we do
What lifts, ennobles, is right and true.
With kindness to all; with malice to none,
That in and through us God's will may be done.
[pg 042]

We venture to make the assertion that there is but one sin: Ignorance and but one salvation: Applied Knowledge . Even the wisest among us know but little of what may be learned, however, and no one has attained to perfection, or can attain in one single short life, but we note that everywhere in nature slow persistent unfoldment makes for higher and higher development of every thing and we call this process evolution.

One of the chief characteristics of evolution lies in the fact that it manifests in alternating periods of activity and rest. The busy summer, when all things upon earth are exerting themselves to bring forth, is followed by the rest and inactivity of winter. The busy day alternates with the quiet of night. The ebb of the ocean is succeeded by the flood-tide. Thus, as all other things move in cycles, the life that expresses itself here upon earth for a few years is not to be thought of as ended when death has been reached, but as surely as the sun rises in the morning after having set at night, will the life that was ended by the death of one body be taken up again in a new vehicle and in a different environment.

[pg 043]

This earth may in fact be likened to a school to which we return life after life to learn new lessons, as our children go to school day after day to increase their knowledge. The child sleeps through the night which intervenes between two days at school and the spirit also has its rest from active life between death and a new birth. There are also different classes in this world-school which correspond to the various grades from kindergarten to college. In the lower classes we find spirits who have gone to the school of life but a few times, they are savages now, but in time they will become wiser and better than we are, and we ourselves shall progress in future lives to spiritual heights of which we cannot even conceive at the present. If we apply ourselves to learn the lessons of life, we shall of course advance much faster in the school of life than if we dilly-dally and idle our time away. This, on the same principle which governs in one of our own institutions of learning.

We are not here then, by the caprice of God. He has not placed one in clover and another in a desert nor has He given one a healthy body so that he may live at ease [pg 044] from pain and sickness, while He placed another in poor circumstances with never a rest from pain. But what we are, we are, on account of our own diligence or negligence, and what we shall be in the future depends upon what we will to be and not upon Divine caprice or upon inexorable fate. No matter what the circumstances, it lies with us to master them, or to be mastered, as we will. Sir Edwin Arnold puts the teaching most beautifully in his "Light of Asia."

" The Books say well, my Brothers! each man's life
The outcome of his former living is;
The bygone wrongs bring forth sorrows and woes
The bygone right breeds bliss.
Each has such lordship as the loftiest ones
Nay for with powers around, above, below
As with all flesh and whatsoever lives
Act maketh joy or woe.

Who toiled a slave may come anew a prince
For gentle worthiness and merit won;
Who ruled a king may wander earth in rags
For things done or undone. "
[pg 045]
Or, as an unknown poet says:
" One ship sails East and another sails West
With the self same winds that blow.
'Tis the set of the sail, and not the gale,
Which determines the way they go.
As the winds of the sea are the ways of fate
As we voyage along through life.
'Tis the act of the soul, which determines the goal
And not the calm or the strife. "

When we wish to engage someone to undertake a certain mission we choose some one whom we think particularly fitted to fulfill the requirements and we must suppose that a Divine Being would use at least as much common sense, and not choose anyone to go his errand who was not fitted therefor. So when we read in the Bible that Samson was foreordained to be the slayer of the Philistines and that Jeremiah was predestined to be a prophet, it is but logical to suppose that they must have been particularly suited to such occupation. John the Baptist also, was born to be a herald of the coming Savior and to preach the kingdom of God which is to take the place of the kingdom of men.
[pg 046]
Had these people had no previous training, how could they have developed such a fitness to fulfill their various missions, and if they had been fitted, how else could they have received their training if not in earlier lives?

The Jews believed in the Doctrine of Rebirth or they would not have asked John the Baptist if he were Elijah, as recorded in the first chapter of John. The Apostles of Christ also held the belief as we may see from the incident recorded in the sixteenth chapter of Matthew where the Christ asked them the question: "Whom do men say that I the Son of Man am?" The Apostles replied: "Some say that Thou art John the Baptist; some, Elias; and others Jeremias or one of the Prophets." Upon this occasion the Christ tacitly assented to the teaching of Rebirth because He did not correct the disciples as would have been His plain duty in His capacity as teacher, when the pupils entertained a mistaken idea.

But to Nicodemus He said unequivocally: "Except a man be born again, he cannot see the kingdom of God" and in the eleventh chapter of Matthew, the fourteenth verse, He said, speaking of John the Baptist: *"this [pg 047] is Elijah ,"* in the seventeenth chapter of Matthew, the twelfth verse, He said: "Elijah has come already and they knew him not, but have done to him whatsoever they listed, . then the disciples understood that he spoke to them of John the Baptist."

Thus we maintain that the Doctrine of Rebirth offers the only solution to the problem of life which is in harmony with the laws of nature, which answers the ethical requirements of the case and permits us to love God without blinding our reason to the inequalities of life and the varying circumstances which give to a few the ease and comfort, the health and wealth, which are denied to the many.

The theory of Heredity advanced by Materialists applies only to the *form* , for as a carpenter uses material from a certain pile of lumber to build a house in which he afterwards lives, so does the spirit take the substance wherewith to build its house from the parents. The carpenter cannot build a house of hard wood from spruce lumber and the spirit also must build a body which is like those from which the material was taken, but the theory of Heredity does not apply upon the moral plane, for it is a notorious fact, that in the rogues galleries of America and [pg 048] Europe there is no case where both father and son are represented. Thus the sons of criminals, though they have the tendencies to crime, keep out of the clutches of the law. Neither will Heredity hold good upon the plane of the intellect, for many cases may be cited where a genius and an idiot spring from the same stock.

The great Cuvier, whose brain was of about the same weight, as Daniel Webster's, and whose intellect was as great, had five children who all died of paresis, the brother of Alexander the Great was an idiot, and thus we hold that another solution must be found to account for the facts of life.

The law of Rebirth coupled with its companion law, the law of Causation does that. When we die after one life, we return to earth later, under circumstances determined by the manner in which we lived before. The gambler is drawn to pool parlors and race tracks to associate with others of like taste, the musician is attracted to the concert halls and music studios, by congenial spirits, and the returning Ego also carries with it its likes and dislikes which cause it to seek parents among the class to which it belongs.

[pg 049]
But then someone will point to cases where we find people of entirely opposite tastes living lives of torture, because grouped in the same family, and forced by circumstances to stay there contrary to their wills. But that does not vitiate the law in the slightest, in each life we contract certain obligations which cannot then be fulfilled. Perhaps we have run away from a duty such as the care of an invalid relative and have met death without coming to a realization of our mistake. That relative upon the other hand may have suffered severely from our neglect, and have stored up a bitterness against us before death terminates the suffering. Death and the subsequent removal to another environment does not pay our debts in this life, any more than the removal from the city where we now live to another place will pay the debts we have contracted prior to our removal. It is therefore quite possible that the two who have injured each other as described, may find themselves members of the same family. Then, whether they remember the past grudge or not, the old enmity will assert itself and cause them to hate anew until the consequent discomfort forces them to tolerate each other, and perhaps [pg 050] later they may learn to love where they hated.

The question also arises in the mind of inquirers: If we have been here before why do we not remember? And the answer is, that while most people are not aware of how their previous existences were spent, there are others who have a very distinct recollection of previous lives. A friend of the writer's for instance, when living in France, one day started to read to her son about a certain city where they were then going upon a bicycle tour, and the boy exclaimed: you do not need to tell me about that mother. I know that city, I lived there and was killed! He then commenced to describe the city and also a certain bridge. Later he took his mother to that bridge and showed her the spot where he had met death centuries before. Another friend travelling in Ireland saw a scene which she recognized and she also described to the party the scene around the bend of the road which she had never seen in this life, so it must have been a memory from a previous life. Numerous other instances could be given where such minor flashes of memory reveal to us glimpses from a past life. The verified case in which a little [pg 051] three year old girl in Santa Barbara described her life and death has been given in the Rosicrucian Cosmo Conception. It is perhaps the most conclusive evidence as it hinges on the veracity of a child too young to have learned deception.

This theory of life does not rest upon speculation however, it is one of the first facts of life demonstrated to the pupil of a Mystery school. He is taught to watch a child in the act of dying, also, to watch it in the invisible world from day to day, until it comes to a new birth a year or two later. Then he knows with absolute certainty that we return to earth to reap in a future life what we now sow.

The reason for taking a child to watch in preference to an adult, is, that the child is reborn very quickly, for its short life on earth has borne but few fruits and these are soon assimilated, while the adult who has lived a long life, and had much experience remains in the invisible worlds for centuries, so that the pupil could not watch him from death to rebirth. The cause of infant mortality will be explained later, here we merely desire to emphasize the fact that it is within the range of possibilities of every one without exception [pg 052] to become able to know at first hand that which is here taught.

The average interval between two earth-lives is about a thousand years. It is determined by the movement of the sun known to astronomers as precession of the equinox, by which the sun moves through one of the signs of the Zodiac in about 2100 years. During that time the conditions upon earth have changed so much that the spirit will find entirely new experiences here, and therefore it returns.

The Great Leaders of evolution always obtain the maximum benefit from each condition designed by them, and as the experiences in the same social conditions are very different in the case of a man from what they are for a woman, the human spirit takes birth twice during the 2100 years measured by the precession of the equinox as already explained, it is born once as a man and another time as a woman. Such is the rule, but it is subject to whatever modifications may be necessary to facilitate reaping what the spirit has sown, as required under the law of Causation which works hand in hand with the law of Rebirth. Thus, at times a spirit may be brought to birth long ere the thousand [pg 053] years have expired, in order to fulfill a certain mission, or it may be detained in the invisible worlds after the time when it should have come to birth according to the strict requirements of a blind law. The laws of nature are not that however. They are Great Intelligences who always subordinate minor considerations to higher ends, and under their beneficent guidance we are constantly progressing from life to life under conditions exactly suited to each individual, until in time we shall attain to a higher evolution and become Supermen.

Oliver Wendell Holmes has so beautifully voiced that aspiration and its con-

summation in the lines:
" Build thee more stately mansions Oh! my soul,
As the swift seasons roll,
Leave thy low-vaulted past;
Let each new temple, nobler than the last,
Shut thee from heaven with a dome more vast.
Till thou at length art free,
Leaving thy outgrown shell by life's unresting sea. "
[pg 054]

Chapter III. The Visible and the Invisible World

The Chemical Region.

If one who is capable of consciously using his spiritual body with the same facility that we now use our physical vehicles should glide away from the earth into interplanetary space, the earth and the various other planets of our solar system would appear to him to be composed of three kinds of matter, roughly speaking. The densest matter, which is our visible earth, would appear to him as being the center of the ball as the yolk is in the center of an egg. Around that nucleus he would observe a finer grade of matter similarly disposed in relation to the central mass, as the white of the egg is disposed outside the yolk. Upon a little closer investigation he would also discover that this second kind of substance permeates the solid [pg 055] earth to the very center, even as the blood percolates through the more solid parts of our flesh. Outside both of these mingling layers of matter he would observe a still finer, third layer corresponding to the shell of the egg, except that this third layer is the finest most subtle of the three grades of matter, and that it inter-penetrates both of the two inner layers.

As already said, the central mass, spiritually seen, is our visible world, composed of solids, liquids and gases. They constitute the earth, its atmosphere, and also the ether, of which physical science speaks hypothetically as permeating the atomic substance of all chemical elements. The second layer of matter is called the Desire World and the outermost layer is called the World of Thought.

A little reflection upon the subject will make clear that just such a constitution is necessary to account for facts of life as we see them. All forms in the world about us are built from chemical substances: solids, liquids and gases, but in so far that they do move, these forms obey a separate and distinct impulse, and when this impelling energy leaves, the form becomes inert. The steam [pg 056] engine rotates under the impetus of an invisible gas called steam. Before steam filled its cylinder, the engine stood still, and when the impelling force is shut off its motion again ceases. The dynamo rotates under the still more subtle influence of an electric current which may also cause the click of a telegraph instrument or the ring of an electric bell, but the dynamo ceases its swift whirl and the persistent ring of the electric bell becomes mute when the invisible electricity is switched off. The form of the bird, the animal and the human being also cease their motion when the inner force which we call *life* has winged its invisible way.

All forms are impelled into motion by desire:—the bird and the animal roam land and air in their desire to secure food and shelter, or for the purpose of breeding, man is also moved by these desires, but has in addition other and higher incentives to spur him to effort, among them is desire for rapidity of motion which led him to construct the steam engine and other devices that move in obedience to *his* desire.

If there were no iron in the mountains man could not build machines. If there were no clay in the soil, the bony structure of the [pg 057] skeleton would be an impossibility, and if there were no Physical World at all, with its solids, liquids and gases, this dense body of ours could never have come into existence. Reasoning along similar lines it must be at once apparent that if there were no Desire World composed of desire-stuff, we should have no way of forming feelings, emotions and desires. A planet composed of the materials we perceive with our *physical* eyes and of no other substances, might be the home of plants which grow unconsciously, but have no desires to cause them to move. The human and animal kingdoms however, would be impossibilities.

Furthermore, there is in the world a vast number of things, from the simplest and most crude instruments, to the most intricate and cunning devices which have been constructed by the hand of man. These reveal the fact of man's thought and ingenuity. Thought must have a source as well as *form* and *feeling* . We saw that it was necessary to have the requisite material in order to build a steam engine or a body and we reasoned from the fact that in order to obtain material to express *desire* there must also be a world composed of desire stuff. Carrying [pg 058] our argument to its logical conclusion, we also hold that unless a World of Thought provides a reservoir of mind stuff upon which we may draw, it would be impossible for us to think and invent the things which we see in even the lowest civilization.

Thus it will be clear that the division of a planet into worlds is not based on fanciful metaphysical speculation, but is logically necessary in the economy of nature. Therefore it must be taken into consideration by any one who would study and aim to understand the inner nature of things. When we see the street cars moving along our streets, it does not explain to say that the motor is driven by electricity of so many amperes at so many volts. These names only add to our confusion until we have thoroughly studied the science of electricity and then we shall find that the mystery deepens, for while the street car belongs to the world of *inert form* perceptible to our vision, the electric current which moves it is indigenous to the realm of *force* , the invisible Desire World, and the thought which created and guides it, comes from the still more subtle World of Thought which is the home world of the human spirit, the Ego.
[pg 059]

It may be objected that this line of argument makes a simple matter exceedingly intricate, but a little reflection will soon show the fallacy of such a contention. Viewed superficially any of the sciences seem extremely simple; anatomically we may divide the body into flesh and bone, chemically we may make the simple divisions between solid, liquid and gas, but to thoroughly master the science of anatomy it is necessary to spend years in close application and learn to know all the little nerves, the ligaments which bind articulations between various parts of the bony structure, to study the several kinds of tissue and their disposition in our system where they form the bones, muscles, glands, etc., which in the aggregate we know as the human body. To properly understand the science of chemistry we must study the valence of the atom which determines the power of combination of the various elements, together with other niceties, such as atomic weight, density, etc. New wonders are constantly opening up to the most experienced chemist, who understands best the immensity of his chosen science.

[pg 060]

The youngest lawyer, fresh from law school knows more about the most intricate cases, in his own estimation, than the judges upon the Supreme Court bench who spend long hours, weeks and months, seriously deliberating over their decisions. But those who, without having studied, think they understand and are fitted to discourse upon the greatest of all sciences, the science of Life and Being, make a greater mistake. After years of patient study, of holy life spent in close application, a man is oftentimes perplexed at the immensity of the subject he studies. He finds it to be so vast in both the direction of the great and small that it baffles description, that language fails, and that the tongue must remain mute. Therefore we hold, (and we speak from knowledge gained through years of close study and investigation), that the finer distinctions which we have made, and shall make, are not at all arbitrary, but absolutely necessary as are divisions and distinctions made in anatomy or chemistry.

No form in the physical world has feeling in the true sense of that word. It is the indwelling life which feels, as we may readily see from the fact that a body which responded [pg 061] to the slightest touch while instinct with life, exhibits no sensation whatever even when cut to pieces after the life has fled. Demonstrations have been made by scientists, particularly by Professor Bose of Calcutta, to show that there is feeling in dead animal tissue and even in tin and other metal, but we maintain that the diagrams which seem to support his contentions in reality demonstrate only a response to impacts similar to the rebound of a rubber ball, and that must not be confused with such feelings as *love*, *hate*, *sympathy* and *aversion*. Goethe also, in his novel "Elective Affinities," (Wahlverwandtschaft), brings out some beautiful illustrations wherein he makes it seem as if atoms loved and hated, from the fact that some elements combine readily while other substances refuse to amalgamate, a phenomenon produced by the different rates of speed at which various elements vibrate and an unequal inclination of their axes. Only where there is sentient life can there be feelings of pleasure and pain, sorrow or joy.

The Etheric Region.

In addition to the solids, liquids and gases which compose the Chemical Region of the [pg 062] Physical World there is also a finer grade of matter called Ether, which permeates the atomic structure of the earth and its atmosphere substantially as science teaches. Scientists have never seen, nor have they weighed, measured or analyzed this substance, but they infer that it must exist in order to account for transmission of light and various other phenomena. If it were possible for us to live in a room from which the air had been exhausted we might speak at the top of our voices, we might ring the largest bell or we might even discharge a cannon close to our ear and we should hear no sound, for air is the medium which transmits sound vibrations to the tympanum of our ear, and that would be lacking. But if an electric light were lighted, we should at once perceive its rays; it would illumine the room despite the lack of air. Hence there must be a substance, capable of being set into vibration, between the electric light and our eyes. That medium scientists call ether, but it is so subtle that no instrument has been devised whereby it may be measured or analyzed and therefore the scientists are without much information concerning it, though forced to postulate its existence.

[pg 063]

We do not seek to belittle the achievements of modern scientists, we have the greatest admiration for them and we entertain high expectations of what ambitions they may yet realize, but we perceive a limitation in the fact, that all discoveries of the past have been made by the invention of wonderful instruments applied in a most ingenious manner to solve seemingly insoluble and baffling problems. The strength of science lies vested in its instruments, for the scientist may say to anyone: Go, procure a number of glasses ground in a certain manner, insert them in a tube, direct that tube toward a certain point in the sky where now nothing appears to your naked eye. You will then see a beautiful star called Uranus. If his directions are followed, anyone is *quickly and without preparation*, able to demonstrate for himself the truth of the scientist's assertion. But while the instruments of science are its tower of strength they also mark the end of its field of investigation, for it is impossible to contact the spirit world with *physical* instruments, so the research of occultists begins where the physical scientist finds his limit and are carried on by *spiritual* means.

[pg 064]

These investigations are as thorough and as reliable as researches by material scientists, but not as easily demonstrable to the general public. Spiritual powers lie dormant within every human being, and when awakened, they compensate for both telescope and microscope, they enable their possessor to investigate, instanter, things beyond the veil of matter, but they are only developed by a patient application and continuance in well doing extended over years, and few are they who have faith to start upon the path to attainment or perseverance to go through with the ordeal. Therefore the occultist's assertions are not generally credited.

We can readily see that long probation must precede attainment, for a person equipped with spiritual sight is able to penetrate walls of houses as easily as we walk through the atmosphere, able to read at will the innermost thoughts of those about him; if not actuated by the most pure and unselfish motives, he would be a scourge to humanity. Therefore that power is safeguarded as we would withhold the dynamite bomb from an anarchist and from the well-intentioned but [pg 065] ignorant person, or, as we withhold match and powder barrel from a child.

In the hands of an experienced engineer the dynamite bomb may be used to open a highway of commerce, and an intelligent farmer may use gunpowder to good account in clearing his field of tree-stumps, but in the hands of an ill-intentioned criminal or ignorant child an explosive may wreck much property and end many lives. The force is the same, but used differently, according to the ability or intention of the user, it may produce results of a diametrically opposite nature. So it is also with spiritual powers, there is a time-lock upon them, as upon a bank safe, which keeps out all until they have earned the privilege and the time is ripe for its exercise.

As already said, the ether is physical matter and responsive to the same laws which govern other physical substances upon this plane of existence. Therefore it requires but a slight extension of *physical* sight to see ether, (which is disposed in four grades of density), the blue haze seen in mountain canyons is in fact ether of the kind known to occult investigators as *"chemical ether."* Many people who see this ether, are unaware [pg 066] that they are possessed of a faculty not enjoyed by all. Others, who have developed spiritual sight are not endowed with etheric vision, a fact which seems an anomaly until the subject of clairvoyance is thoroughly understood.

The reason is, that as ether is physical matter, etheric sight depends upon the sensitiveness of the optic nerve while spiritual sight is acquired by developing latent vibratory powers in two little organs situated in the brain: the Pituitary body and the Pineal gland. Nearsighted people even, may have etheric vision. Though unable to read the print in a book, they may be able to "see through a wall," owing to the fact that their optic nerve responds more rapidly to fine than to coarse vibrations.

When anyone views an object with etheric sight he sees *through* that object in a manner similar to the way an x-ray penetrates opaque substances. If he looks at a sewing machine, he will perceive, first an outer casing; then, the works within, and behind both, the casing furthest away from him.

If he has developed the grade of spiritual vision which opens the Desire World to him and he looks at the same object, he will [pg 067] see it both inside and out. If he looks closely, he will perceive every little atom spinning upon its axis and no part or particle will be excluded from his perception.

But if his spiritual sight has been developed in such a measure that he is capable of viewing the sewing machine with the vision peculiar to the World of Thought, he will behold a cavity where he had previously seen the form.

Things seen with etheric vision are very much alike in color, they are nearly reddish-blue, purple or violet, according to the density of the ether, but when we view any object with the spiritual sight pertaining to the Desire World, it scintillates and coruscates in a thousand ever changing colors so indescribably beautiful that they can only be compared to living fire, and the writer therefore calls this grade of vision color sight, but when the spiritual vision of the World of Thought is the medium of perception, the seer finds that in addition to still more beautiful colors, there issues from the cavity described a constant flow of a certain harmonious *tone*. Thus this world wherein we now consciously live and which we perceive by means of our physical senses is preeminently [pg 068] the world of *form*, the Desire World is particularly the world of *color* and the World of Thought is the realm of *tone*.

Because of the relative proximity or distance of these worlds, a statue, a *form*, withstands the ravages of time for millenniums, but the *colors* upon a painting fade in far shorter time, for they come from the Desire World, and *music* which is native to the World furthest removed from us, the World of Thought, is like a will-o-the-wisp which none may catch or hold, it is gone again as soon as it has made its appearance. But there is in color and music a compensation for this increasing evanescence.

The statue is cold and dead as the mineral of which it is composed and has attractions for but few though its *form is* a tangible reality.

The forms upon a painting are illusory yet they express *life*, on account of the *color* which has come from a region where nothing is inert and lifeless. Therefore the painting is enjoyed by many.

Music is intangible and ephemeral, but it comes from the home world of the spirit and though so fleeting it is recognized by the spirit as a *soul-speech* fresh from the celestial [pg 069] realms, an echo from the home whence we are now exiled, and therefore it touches a cord in our being, regardless of whether we realize the true cause or not.

Thus we see that there are various grades of spiritual sight, each suited to the superphysical realm which it opens to our perception: Etheric vision, color vision and tonal vision.

The occult investigator finds that ether is of four kinds, or grades of density:

The Chemical Ether,
The Life Ether,
The Light Ether,
The Reflecting Ether.

The Chemical Ether is the avenue of expression for forces promoting assimilation, growth and the maintenance of form.

The Life Ether is the vantage ground of forces active in propagation, or the building of new forms.

The Light Ether transmits the motive power of the sun along the various nerves of *living* bodies and makes motion possible.

The Reflecting Ether receives an impression of all that is, lives and moves. It also [pg 070] records each change, in a similar manner as the film upon a moving picture machine. In this record mediums and psychometrists may read the past, upon the same principle as, under proper conditions, moving pictures are reproduced time and again.

We have been speaking of ether as an avenue of *forces*, a word which conveys no meaning to the average mind, because force is invisible. But to an occult investigator the forces are not merely names such as steam, electricity, etc. He finds them to be intelligent beings of varying grades, both sub and superhuman. What we call "laws of nature," are great intelligences which guide more elemental beings in accordance with certain rules designed to further their evolution.

In the Middle Ages, when many people were still endowed with a remnant of *negative* clairvoyance, they spoke of Gnomes and Elves or Fairies, which roamed about the mountains and forests. These were the *earth* spirits. They also told of the Undine or *water*-sprite, which inhabited rivers and streams, of Sylphs which were said to dwell in the mists above moat and moor, as air spirits, but not much was said of the Salamanders, [pg 071] as they are, fire spirits, and therefore not so easily detected, or so readily accessible to the majority of people.

The old folk stories are now regarded as superstitions, but as a matter of fact, one endowed with etheric vision may yet perceive the little gnomes building green chlorophyll into the leaves of plants and giving to flowers the multiplicity of delicate tints which delight our eyes.

Scientists have attempted time and again to offer an adequate explanation of the phenomenon of wind and storm but have failed signally, nor can they succeed while they seek a mechanical solution to what is really a manifestation of life. Could they see the hosts of sylphs winging their way hither and thither, they would *know* who and what is responsible for the fickleness of the wind; could they watch a storm at sea from the etheric view-point they would perceive that the saying "the war of the elements" is not an empty phrase, for the heaving sea is truly then a battlefield of sylphs and undines and the howling tempest is the war cry of spirits in the air.

Also the salamanders are found everywhere and no fire is lighted without their [pg 072] help, but they are mostly active underground. They are responsible for explosions and volcanic eruptions.

The classes of beings which we have mentioned are still sub-human, but will all at some time reach a stage in evolution corresponding to the human, though under different circumstances from those under which we evolve. But at present the wonderful intelligences we speak of as the laws of nature, marshall the armies of less evolved entities mentioned.

To arrive at a better understanding of what these various beings are, and their relation to us, we may take an illustration: Let us suppose that a mechanic is making an engine, and meanwhile a dog is watching him. It *sees* the man at his labor, and how he uses various tools to shape his materials, also how, from the crude iron, steel, brass and other metals the engine slowly takes shape. The dog is a being from a lower evolution and does not comprehend the purpose of the mechanic but it *sees* both the workman, his labor and the result thereof, which manifests as an engine.

Let us now suppose that the dog were able to see the materials which slowly [pg 073] change their shape, assemble and become an engine but that it is unable to perceive the workman and to see the work he does. The dog would then be in the same relation to the mechanic as we are to the great intelligences we call laws of nature, and their assistants, the nature spirits, for we behold the manifestations of their work as *force* moving matter in various ways but always under immutable conditions.

In the ether we may also observe the angels, whose densest body is made of that material, as our dense body is formed of gases, liquids and solids. These beings are one step beyond the human stage, as we are a degree in advance of the animal evolution. We have never been animals like our present fauna, however, but at a previous stage in the development of our planet we had an animal-like constitution. Then the angels were human, though they have never possessed a dense body such as ours, nor ever functioned in any material denser than ether. At some time, in a future condition, the earth will again become ethereal. Then man will be *like* the angels. Therefore the Bible tells us that man was made *a little while* lower than the angels (Paul's letter to [pg 074] the Hebrews, second chapter, seventh verse; see marginal reading.)

As ether is the avenue of vital, creative forces, and as angels are such expert builders of ether, we may readily understand that they are eminently fitted to be warders of the propagative forces in plant, animal and man. All through the Bible we find them thus engaged: Two *angels* came to Abraham and announced the birth of Isaac, they *promised* a child to the man who had obeyed God. Later *these same angels* destroyed Sodom for *abuse of the creative force*. Angels foretold *to the parents* of Samuel and Samson, the birth of these giants of brain and brawn. To Elizabeth came the *angel* (not archangel) Gabriel and announced the birth of John, later he appeared also to Mary with the message that she was chosen to bear Jesus.

The Desire World.

When spiritual sight is developed so that it becomes possible to behold the Desire World, many wonders confront the newcomer, for conditions are so widely different from what they are here, that a description must sound quite as incredible as a fairy tale to anyone who has not himself seen them. [pg 075] Many cannot even believe that such a world exists, and that other people can see that which is invisible to them, yet some people are blind to the beauties of this world which we see. A man who was born blind, may say to us: I know that this world exists, I can hear, I can smell, I can taste and above all I can feel but when you speak of light and of color, they are nonexistent to me. You say that you *see* these things, I cannot believe it for I cannot *see* myself. You say that light and color are all about me, but none of the senses at my command reveal them to me and I do not believe that the sense you call *sight* exists. I think you suffer from hallucinations. We might sympathize very sincerely with the poor man who is thus afflicted, but his scepticism, reasonings and objections and sneers notwithstanding we would be obliged to maintain that we perceive light and color.

The man whose spiritual sight has been awakened is in a similar position with respect to those who do not perceive the Desire World of which he speaks. If the blind man acquires the faculty of sight by an operation, his eyes are opened and he will be compelled to assert the existence of light and [pg 076] color which he formerly denied, and when spiritual sight is acquired by anyone, he also perceives for himself the facts related by others. Neither is it an argument against the existence of spiritual realms that seers are at variance in their descriptions of conditions in the invisible world. We need but to look into books on travel, and compare stories brought home by explorers of China, India or Africa and we shall find them differing widely and often contradictory, because each traveler saw things from his own standpoint, under other conditions than those met by his brother authors, and we maintain that the man who has read most widely these varying tales concerning a certain Country *and wrestled with the contradictions of narrators*, will have a more comprehensive idea of the country or people of whom he has read, than the man who has only read one story assented to by all the authors. Similarly, the varying stories of visitors to the Desire World are of value, because giving a fuller view, and more rounded, than if all had seen things from the same angle.

In this world matter and force are widely different. The chief characteristic of matter here is *inertia* : the tendency to remain at [pg 077] rest until acted upon by a force which sets it in motion. In the Desire World, on the contrary, force and matter are almost indistinguishable one from the other. We might almost describe desire-stuff as force-matter, for it is in incessant motion, responsive to the slightest *feeling* of a vast multitude of beings which populate this wonderful world in nature. We often speak of the "teeming millions" of China and India, even of our vast cities, London, New York, Paris or Chicago, we consider them overcrowded in the extreme, yet even the densest population of any spot upon earth is sparsely inhabited compared with the crowded conditions of the Desire World. No inconvenience is felt by any of the denizens of that realm, however, for, while in this world two things cannot occupy the same space at the same time, it is different there. A number of people and things may exist *in the same place at the same time* and be engaged in most diverse activities, regardless of what others are doing, such is the wonderful elasticity of desire stuff. As an illustration we may mention a case where the writer while attending religious service, plainly perceived at the altar certain beings interested in furthering that [pg 078] service and working to achieve that end. At the same time there drifted through the room and the altar, a table at which four persons were engaged in playing cards. They were as oblivious to the existence of the beings engaged in furthering our religious service, as though these did not exist.

The Desire World is the abode of those who have died, for some time subsequent to that event, and we may mention in the above connection that the so-called "dead" very often stay for a long while among their still living friends. Unseen by their relatives they go about the familiar rooms. At first they are often unaware of the condition mentioned: "that two persons may be in the same place at the same time," and when they seat themselves in a chair or at the table, a living relative may take the supposedly vacant seat. The man we mistakenly call dead will at first hurry out of his seat to escape being sat upon, but he soon learns that being sat upon does not hurt him in his altered condition, and that he may remain in his chair regardless of the fact that his living relative is also sitting there.

In the lower regions of the Desire World the whole body of each being may be seen, but [pg 079] in the highest regions only the head seems to remain. Raphael, who like many other people in the middle ages was gifted with a so-called *second sight* , pictured that condition for us in his Sistine Madonna, now in the Dresden Art Gallery, where Madonna and the Christchild are represented as floating in a golden atmosphere and surrounded by a host of genie-heads: conditions which the occult investigator knows to be in harmony with actual facts.

Among the entities who are, so to speak, "*native* " to that realm of nature, none are perhaps better known to the Christian world than the Archangels. These exalted Beings were human at a time in the earth's history when we were yet plant-like. Since then we have advanced two steps: through the animal and to the human stage of development. The present Archangels have also made two steps in progression; one, in which they were similar to what the angels are now, and another step which made them what we call Archangels.

Their densest body, though differing from ours in shape, and made of desire stuff, is used by them as a vehicle of consciousness in the same manner that we use our body. They [pg 080] are expert manipulators of forces in the Desire World, and these forces, as we shall see, move all the world to action. Therefore the Archangels work with humanity *industrially* and *politically* as arbitrators of the destiny of peoples and nations. The Angels may be said to be *family* -spirits whose mission is to unite a few spirits as members of a family, and cement them with ties of blood and love of kin, while the Archangels may be called race and national spirits, as they unite whole nations by patriotism or love of home and country. They are responsible for the rise and fall of nations, they give war or peace, victory or defeat as it serves the best interests of the people they rule. This we may see, for instance, from the book of Daniel, where the Archangel Michael (not to be confounded with the Michael, who is ambassador from the sun to the earth), is called the prince of the children of Israel. Another Archangel tells Daniel, (in the tenth chapter) that he intends to fight the prince of Persia by means of the Greeks.

There are varying grades of intelligence among human beings, some are qualified to hold high and lofty positions entirely beyond the ability of others. So it is also among [pg 081] higher beings, not all Archangels are fitted to govern a nation and rule the destiny of a race, people or tribe, some are not fitted to rule human beings at all, but as the animals also have a desire nature these lower grades of Archangels govern the animals as group-spirits and evolve to higher capacity thereby.

The work of the race spirits is readily observable in the people it governs. The lower in the scale of evolution the people, the more they show a certain racial likeness. That is due to the work of the race spirit. One national spirit is responsible for the swarthy complexion common to Italians, for instance, while another causes the Scandinavians to be blond. In the more advanced types of humanity there is a wider divergence from the common type, due to the individualized Ego, which thus expresses in form and feature its own particular idiosyncrasies. Among the lower types of humanity such as Mongolians, native African Negroes and South Sea Islanders, the resemblance of individuals in each tribe makes it almost impossible for civilized Westerners to distinguish between them. Among animals, where the separate spirit is not individualized and self-conscious, the resemblance is not only much more [pg 082] marked physically but extends even to traits and characteristics. We may write the biography of a man, for the experiences of each varies from that of others and his acts are different, but we cannot write the biography of an animal for members of each tribe all act alike under similar circumstances. If we desire to know the facts about Edward VII, it would profit us nothing to study the life of the Prince-Consort, his father, or of George V, his son, as both would be entirely different from Edward. In order to find out what manner of man he was, we must study his own individual life. If, on the other hand, we wish to know the characteristics of beavers, we may observe any individual of the tribe, and when we have studied its idiosyncrasies, we shall know the traits of the whole tribe of beavers. What we call "instinct," is in reality the dictates of group-spirits which govern separate individuals of its tribe telepathically, as it were.

The ancient Egyptians knew of these animal group spirits and sketched many of them, in a crude way, upon their temples and tombs. Such figures with a human body and an animal head actually live in the desire world. They may be spoken to, and will be [pg 083] found much more intelligent than the average human being.

That statement brings up another peculiarity of conditions in the Desire World in respect of language. Here in this World human speech is so diversified that there are countries where people who live only a few miles apart speak a dialect so different that they understand each other with great difficulty, and each nation has its own language that varies altogether from the speech of other peoples.

In the lower Regions of the Desire World, there is the same diversity of tongues as on earth, and the so-called "dead" of one nation find it impossible to converse with those who lived in another country. Hence linguistic accomplishments are of great value to the "Invisible Helpers", of whom we shall hear later, as their sphere of usefulness is enormously extended by that ability.

Even apart from difference of language our mode of speech is exceedingly productive of misunderstandings. The same words often convey most opposite ideas to different minds. If we speak of a "body of water", one person may think we mean a lake of small dimensions, the thoughts of another may be [pg 084] directed to the great American Lakes and a third person's thoughts may be turned towards the Atlantic or Pacific Oceans. If we speak of a "light", one may think of a gas-light, another of an electric Arc-lamp, or if we say "red", one person may think we mean a delicate shade of pink and another gets the idea of crimson. The misunderstandings of what words mean goes even farther, as illustrated in the following.

The writer once opened a reading room in a large city where he lectured, and invited his audience to make use thereof. Among those who availed themselves of the opportunity was a gentleman who had for many years been a veritable "metaphysical tramp," roaming from lecture to lecture, hearing the teachings of everybody and practicing nothing. Like the Athenians on Mars' Hill, he was always looking for something "new," particularly in the line of phenomena, and his mind was in that seething chaotic state which is one of the most prominent symptoms of "mental indigestion."

Having attended a number of our lectures he knew from the program that: "The lecturer does not give readings, or cast horoscopes *for pay* ." But seeing on the door of [pg 085] the newly opened reading room, the legend: "Free Reading Room," his erratic mind at once jumped to the conclusion that although we were opposed to telling fortunes for pay, we were now going to give free readings of the future in the Free Reading Room. He was much disappointed that we did not intend to tell fortunes, either gratis or for a consideration, and we changed our sign to "Free Library" in order to obviate a repetition of the error.

In the higher Regions of the Desire

World the confusion of tongues gives place to a universal mode of expression which absolutely prevents misunderstandings of our meaning. There each of our thoughts takes a definite form and color perceptible to all, and this thought-symbol emits a certain tone, which is not a word, but it conveys our meaning to the one we address no matter what language he spoke on earth.

To arrive at an understanding of how such a universal language becomes possible and is at once comprehended by all, without preparation, we may take as an illustration the manner in which a musician reads music. A German or a Polish composer may write an opera. Each has his own peculiar terminology [pg 086] and expresses it in his own language. When that opera is to be played by an Italian band master, or by a Spanish or American musician, it need not be translated, the notes and symbols upon the page are a universally understood language of symbols which is intelligible to musicians of no matter what nationality. Similarly with figures, the German counts: ein, zwei, drei; the Frenchman says: un, deux, trois, and in English we use the words: one, two, three, but the figures: 1, 2, 3, though differently spoken, are intelligible to all and mean the same. There is no possibility of misunderstanding in the cases of either music or figures. Thus it is also with the universal language peculiar to the higher Regions of the Desire World and the still more subtle realms in nature, it is intelligible to all, an exact mode of expression.

Returning to our description of the entities commonly met with in the lower Desire World, we may note that other systems of religion than the Egyptian, already mentioned, have spoken of various classes of beings native to these realms. The Zoroastrian Religion, for instance, mentions Seven Ameshaspends and the Izzards as having dominion over certain days in the month and certain months in [pg 087] the year. The Christian religion speaks of Seven Spirits before the Throne, which are the same beings the Persians called Ameshaspends. Each of them rules over two months in the year while the seventh: Michael, the highest, is their leader, for he is ambassador from the sun to the earth, the others are ambassadors from the planets. The Catholic religion with its abundant occult information takes most notice of these "*star-angels*" and knows considerable about their influence upon the affairs of the earth.

The Ameshaspends, however, do not inhabit the lower Regions of the Desire World but influence the Izzards. According to the old Persian legend these beings are divisible into one group of twenty-eight classes, and another group of three classes. Each of these classes has dominion over, or takes the lead of all the other classes on one certain day of the month. They regulate the weather conditions on that day and work with animal and man in particular. At least the twenty-eight classes do that, the other group of three classes has nothing to do with animals, because they have only twenty-eight pair of spinal nerves, while human beings have thirty-one. Thus animals are attuned to the lunar month of [pg 088] twenty-eight days, while man is correlated to the solar month of thirty or thirty-one days. The ancient Persians were astronomers but not physiologists, they had no means of knowing the different nervous constitution of animal and man, but they saw clairvoyantly these superphysical beings, they noted and recorded their work with animal and men and our own anatomical investigations may show us the reason for these divisions of the classes of Izzards recorded in that ancient system of philosophy.

Still another class of beings should be mentioned: those who have entered the Desire World through the gate of death and are now hidden from our physical vision. These so-called "dead" are in fact much more alive than any of us, who are tied to a dense body and subject to all its limitations, who are forced to slowly drag this clog along with us at the rate of a few miles an hour, who must expend such an enormous amount of energy upon propelling that vehicle that we are easily and quickly tired, even when in the best of health and who are often confined to a bed, sometimes for years, by the indisposition of this heavy mortal coil. But when that is once shed and the freed spirit [pg 089] can again function in its spiritual body, sickness is an unknown condition and distance is annihilated, or at least practically so, for though it was necessary for the Savior to liken the freed spirit to the wind which blows where it listeth, that simile gives but a poor description of what actually takes place in soul flights. Time is nonexistent there, as we shall presently explain, so the writer has never been able to time himself, but has on several occasions timed others when he was in the physical body and they speeding through space upon a certain errand. Distances such as from the Pacific Coast to Europe, the delivery of a short message there and the return to the body has been accomplished in slightly less than one minute. Therefore our assertion, that those whom we call dead are in reality much more alive than we, is well founded in facts.

We spoke of the dense body in which we now live, as a "clog" and a "fetter." It must not be inferred, however, that we sympathize with the attitude of certain people who, when they have learned with what ease soul-flights are accomplished, go about bemoaning the fact that they are now imprisoned. They are constantly thinking of, and longing for, the day [pg 090] when they shall be able to leave this mortal coil behind and fly away in their spiritual body. Such an attitude of mind is decidedly mistaken, the great and wise beings who are invisible leaders of our evolution have not placed us here to no purpose. Valuable lessons are to be learned in this visible world wherein we dwell, that cannot be learned in any other realm of nature, and the very conditions of density and inertia whereof such people complain, are factors which make it possible to acquire the knowledge this world is designed to give. This fact was so amply illustrated in a recent experience of the writer:—A friend had been studying occultism for a number of years but had not studied astrology.

Last year she became aroused to the importance of this branch of study as a key to self knowledge and a means of understanding the natures of others, also of developing the compassion for their errors, so necessary in the cultivation of love of one's neighbor. Love of our neighbor the Savior enjoined upon us as the Supreme Commandment which is the fulfillment of all laws, and as Astrology teaches us to *bear* and *forbear*, it helps as nothing else can in the development [pg 091] of the supreme virtue. She therefore joined one of the classes started in Los Angeles by the writer, but a sudden illness quickly ended in death and thus terminated her study of the subject in the physical body, ere it was well begun.

Upon one of many occasions when she visited the writer subsequent to her release from the body, she deplored the fact that it seemed so difficult to make headway in her study of astrology. The writer advised continued attendance at the classes, and suggested that she could surely get someone "on the other side" to help her study.

At this she exclaimed impatiently: "Oh yes! of course I attend the classes, I have done so right along; I have also found a friend who helps me here. But you cannot imagine how difficult it is to concentrate here upon mathematical calculations and the judgment of a horoscope or in fact upon any subject here, where every little thought-current takes you miles away from your study. I used to think it difficult to concentrate when I had a physical body, but it is not a circumstance to the obstacles which face the student here."

[pg 092]

The physical body was an anchor to her, and it is that to all of us. Being dense, it is also to a great extent impervious to disturbing influences from which the more subtle spiritual bodies do not shield us. It enables us to bring our ideas to a logical conclusion with far less effort at concentration than is necessary in that realm where all is in such incessant and turbulent motion. Thus we are gradually developing the faculty of holding our thoughts to a center by existence in this world, and we should value our opportunities here, rather than deplore the limitations which help in one direction more than they fetter in another. In fact, we should never deplore any condition, each has its lesson. If we try to learn what that lesson is and to assimilate the experience which may be extracted therefrom, we are wiser than those who waste time in vain regrets.

We said there is no time in the Desire World, and the reader will readily understand that such must be the case from the fact, already mentioned, that nothing there is opaque.

In this world the rotation of the opaque earth upon its axis is responsible for the alternating conditions of day and night. We [pg 093] call it Day—when the spot where we live is turned towards the sun and its rays illumine our environment, but when our home is turned away from the sun and its rays obstructed by the opaque earth we term the resulting darkness: Night. The passage of the earth in its orbit around the sun produces the seasons and the year, which are our divisions of time. But in the Desire World where all is light there is but one long day. The spirit is not there fettered by a heavy physical body, so it does not need sleep and existence is unbroken. Spiritual substances are not subject to contraction and expansion such as arise here from heat and cold, hence summer and winter are also non-existent. Thus there is nothing to differentiate one moment from another in respect of the conditions of light and darkness, summer and winter, which mark time for us. Therefore, while the so-called "dead" may have a very accurate memory of time as regards the life they lived here in the body, they are usually unable to tell anything about the chronological relation of events which have happened to them in the Desire World, and it is a very common thing to find that they do not even know how many years have elapsed since [pg 094] they passed out from this plane of existence. Only students of the Stellar Science are able to calculate the passage of time after their demise.

When the occult investigator wishes to study an event in the past history of man, he may most readily call up the picture from *the memory of nature*, but if he desires to fix the time of the incident, he will be obliged to count backwards by the motion of the heavenly bodies. For that purpose he generally uses the measure provided by the sun's precession: Each year the sun crosses the earth's equator about the twenty-first of March. Then day and night are of even length, therefore this is called the Vernal equinox. But on account of a certain wabbling motion of the earth's axis, the sun does not cross over at the same place in the Zodiac, it reaches the equator a little too early, it *precedes*, year by year it moves *backwards* a little. At the time of the birth of Christ, for instance, the Vernal Equinox was in about seven degrees of the Zodiacal sign Aries. During the two thousand years which intervene between that event and the present time, the sun has moved *backwards* about twenty-seven degrees, so that it is now in about ten degrees [pg 095] of the sign Pisces. It moves around the whole circle of the Zodiac in about 25,868 years. The occult investigator may therefore count back the number of signs, or whole circles, which the sun has *preceded* between the present day and the time of the event he is investigating. Thus he has by the use of the heavenly time keepers a very approximately correct measure of time even though he is in the Desire World and that is another reason for studying the Stellar Science.

The World of Thought.

When we have attained the spiritual development necessary to consciously enter the World of Thought and leave the Desire World, which is the realm of light and color, we pass through a condition which the occult investigator calls The Great Silence.

As previously stated, the higher Regions of the Desire World exhibit the marked peculiarity of blending form and sound, but when one passes through the Great Silence, all the world seems to disappear and the spirit has the feeling of floating in an ocean of intense light, utterly alone, yet absolutely fearless, since unimbued with a sense of its form or sound, nor past or future, but all is [pg 096] one eternal NOW. There seems to be neither pleasure nor pain and yet there is no absence of feeling but it all seems to center in the one idea:— "*I am*"! The human Ego stands face to face with itself as it were, and for the time being all else is shut out. This is the experience of anyone who passes that breach between the Desire World and the World of Thought, whether involuntarily, in the course of an ordinary cyclic pilgrimage of the soul, which we shall later elucidate when speaking of the post-mortem existence, or by an act of the will, as in the case of the trained occult investigator, all have the same experience in transition.

There are two main divisions in the Physical World: the Chemical Region and the Etheric Region. The World of Thought also has two great subdivisions: The Region of concrete Thought and the Region of abstract Thought.

As we specialize the material of the Physical World and shape into a dense body, and as we form the force-matter of the Desire World into a desire body, so do we appropriate a certain amount of mindstuff from the Region of concrete Thought; but we, as spirits, [pg 097] clothe ourselves in spirit-substance from the Region of abstract Thought and thereby we become individual, separate Egos.

The Region of Concrete Thought.

The Region of concrete Thought is neither shadowy nor illusory. It is the acme of reality and this world which we mistakenly regard as the only verity, is but an evanescent replica of that Region.

A little reflection will show the reasonableness of this statement and prove our contention that all we see here is really crystallized thought. Our houses, our machinery, our chairs and tables, all that has been made by the hand of man is the embodiment of a thought. As the juices in the soft body of the snail gradually crystallize into the hard and flinty shell which it carries upon its back and which hides it, so everything used in our civilization is a concretion of invisible, intangible mind-stuff. The thought of James Watt in time congealed into a steam engine and revolutionized the world. Edison's thought was condensed into an electric generator which has turned night to day, and had it not been for the thought of Morse and Marconi, the telegraph would not have annihilated [pg 098] distance as it does today. An earthquake may wreck a city and demolish the lighting plant and telegraph station, but the thoughts of Watt, Edison and Morse remain, and upon the basis of their indestructible ideas new machinery may be constructed and operations resumed. Thus thoughts are more permanent than things.

The sensitive ear of the musician detects a certain musical note in every city which is different from that of another city. He hears in each little brook a new melody, and to him the sound of wind in the treetops of different forests give a varying sound. In the Desire World we noted the existence of forms similar to the shapes of things here, also that seemingly *sound proceeds from form* , but in the Region of concrete Thought it is different, for while each form occupies and obscures a certain space here, form is nonexistent when viewed from the standpoint of the Region of concrete Thought. Where the form was, a transparent, vacuous space is observable. *From that empty void comes a sound* which is the "keynote" that *creates* and maintains the *form* whence it *appears* to come, as the almost invisible core of a gas-flame is the source of the light we perceive.
[pg 099]
Sound from a vacuum cannot be heard in the Physical World, but the harmony which proceeds from the vacuous cavity of a celestial *archetype* is "the voice of the silence," and it becomes audible when all earthly sounds have ceased. Elijah heard it not while the storm was raging; nor was it in evidence during the turbulence of the earthquake, nor in the crackling and roaring fire, but when the destructive and inharmonious sounds of this world had melted into silence, "the still small voice" issued its commands to save Elijah's life.

That "keynote" is a direct manifestation of the Higher Self which uses it to impress and govern the Personality it has created. But alas, part of its life has been infused into the material side of its being, which has thus obtained a certain will of its own and only too often are the two sides of our nature at war.

At last there comes a time when the spirit is too weary to strive with the recalcitrant flesh, when "the voice of the silence" ceases.

The earthly nourishment we may seek to give, will not avail to sustain a form when this harmonious sound, this "word from heaven" no longer reverberates through the empty void of the celestial archetype, [pg 100] for "man lives not by bread alone," but by the WORD, and the last sound-vibration of the "keynote" is the death-knell of the physical body.

In this world we are compelled to investigate and to study a thing before we know about it, and although the facilities for gaining information are in some respects much greater in the Desire World, a certain amount of investigation is necessary nevertheless to acquire knowledge. In the World of Thought, on the contrary, it is different. When we wish to know about any certain thing there, and we turn our attention thereto, then that thing speaks to us, as it were. The sound it emits at once gives us a most luminous comprehension of every phase of its nature. We attain to a realization of its past history; the whole story of its unfoldment is laid bare and we seem to have lived through all of those experiences together with the thing we are investigating.

Were it not for one enormous difficulty, the story thus obtained would be exceedingly valuable. But all this information, this life-picture, flows in upon us with an enormous rapidity in a moment, in the twinkling of an eye, so that it has neither beginning nor end, [pg 101] for, as said, in the World of Thought, all is one great NOW, Time does not exist.

Therefore, when we want to use the archetypal information in the Physical World, we must disentangle and arrange it in chronological order with beginning and ending before it becomes intelligible to beings living in a realm where Time is a prime factor. That rearrangement is a most difficult task as all words are coined with relation to the three dimensions of space and the evanescent unit of time, the fleeting moment, hence much of that information remains unavailable.

Among the denizens of this Region of concrete Thought we may note particularly two classes. One is called the powers of darkness by Paul and the mystic investigator of the Western World knows them as Lords of Mind. They were human at the time when the earth was in a condition of darkness such as worlds in the making go through before they become luminous and reach the firemist-stage. At that time we were in our mineral evolution. That is to say: The Human Spirit which has now awakened was encrusted in the ball of mind-stuff, which was then the earth. At that time the present Human Spirits were as much asleep as is the life which [pg 102] ensouls our minerals of today, and as we are working with the mineral chemical constituents of the earth, molding them into houses, railways, steam-boats, chairs, etc, etc., so those beings, who are now Lords of Mind, worked with us when we were mineral-like. They have since advanced three steps, through stages similar to that of the Angels and Archangels, before they attained their present position and became creative intelligences. They are expert builders of mind stuff, as we are builders of the present mineral substances and therefore they have given us necessary help to acquire a mind which is the highest development of the human being.

According to the foregoing explanation it seems to be an anomaly when Paul speaks of them as evil and exhorts us to withstand them. The difficulty disappears, however, when we understand that good and evil are but relative qualities. An illustration will make the point clear:—Let us suppose that an expert organ builder has constructed a wonderful organ, a masterpiece. Then he has followed his vocation in the proper manner, and is therefore to be commended for the good which he has done. But if he is not satisfied to leave well enough alone, if he refuses [pg 103] to give up his product to the musician who understands how to play upon the instrument; if he intrudes his presence into the concert hall, he is out of place and to be censured as evil. Similarly the Lords of Mind did the greatest possible service to humanity when they helped us to acquire our mind, but many subtle thought influences come from them, and are to be resisted, as Paul very properly emphasizes.

The other class of beings which must be mentioned are called Archetypal Forces by the Western School of occultism. They direct the energies of the creative Archetypes native to this realm. They are a composite class of beings of many different grades of intelligences, and there is one stage in the cyclic journey of the Human Spirit when that also labors in, and is part of, that great host of beings. For the Human Spirit is also destined to become a great creative intelligence at some future time, and if there were no school wherein it could gradually learn to create, it would not be able to advance, for nothing in nature is done suddenly. An acorn planted in the soil does not become a majestic oak over night, but many years of slow, persistent growth are required before [pg 104] it attains to the stature of a giant of the forest. A man does not become an Angel by the mere fact of dying and entering a new world any more than an animal advances to be a man by the same process. But in time all that lives, mounts the ladder of Being from the clod to the God. There is no limitation possible to the spirit, and so at various stages in its unfoldment the Human Spirit works with the other nature forces, according to the stage of intelligence which it has attained. It creates, changes and remodels the earth upon which it is to live. Thus, under the great law of cause and effect, which we observe in every realm of nature, it reaps upon earth what it has sown in heaven, and vice versa. It grows slowly but persistently and advances continually.

The Region of Abstract Thought.

Various religious systems have been given to humanity at different times, each suited to meet the spiritual needs of the people among whom it was promulgated, and, coming from the same divine source:—God, all religions exhibit similar fundamentals or first principles.

All systems teach that there was a time when *darkness* reigned supreme. Everything [pg 105] which we now perceive was then non-existent. Earth, sky and the heavenly bodies were uncreate, so were the multitudinous forms which live and move upon the various planets.—All, all, was yet in a fluidic condition and the Universal Spirit brooded *quiescent* in limitless Space as the One Existence.

The Greeks called that condition of homogeneity Chaos , and the state of orderly segregation which we now see; the marching orbs which illumine the vaulted canopy of heaven, the stately procession of planets around a central light, the majestic sun; the unbroken sequence of the seasons and the unvarying alternation of tidal ebb and flow;—all this aggregate of systematic order, was called Cosmos , and was supposed to have proceeded from Chaos.

The Christian Mystic obtains a deeper comprehension when he opens his Bible and ponders the first five verses of that brightest gem of all spiritual lore: the Gospel of St. John.

As he reverently opens his aspiring heart to acquire understanding of those sublime mystical teachings he transcends the form-side of nature, comprising various realms of which we have been speaking, and finds himself [pg 106] "in the spirit," as did the prophets in olden times. He is then in the Region of abstract Thought and sees the eternal verities which also Paul beheld in this, the third, heaven.

For those among us who are unable to obtain knowledge save by reasoning upon the matter, however, it will be necessary to examine the fundamental meaning of words used by St. John to clothe his wonderful teaching, which was originally given in the Greek language, a much simpler matter than is commonly supposed, for Greek words have been freely introduced into our modern languages, particularly in scientific terms, and we shall show how this ancient teaching is supported by the latest discoveries of modern science.

The opening verse of the gospel of St. John is as follows: "In the *beginning* was the *Word*, and the *Word* was with *God*, and the *Word* was *God*." We will examine the words: "beginning," "Word" and "God." We may also note that in the Greek version the concluding sentence reads: "and God was the Word," a difference which makes a great distinction.

[pg 107]

It is an axiomatic truth that "out of nothing, nothing comes," and it has often been asserted by scoffers that the Bible teaches generation "from nothing." We readily agree that *translations* into the modern languages promulgate this erroneous doctrine, but we have shown in The Rosicrucian Cosmo Conception (chapter on "the Occult Analysis of Genesis"), that the Hebrew text speaks of an *ever-existing essence*, as the basis whence all forms, the earth and the heavenly lights included, were first created, and John also gives the same teaching.

The Greek word arche, in the opening sentence of the gospel of St. John has been translated the beginning, and it may be said to have that meaning, but it also has other valid interpretations, vastly more significant of the idea John wished to convey. It means:—an elementary condition,—a chief source,—a first principle,—primordial matter.

There was a time when science insisted that the elements were immutable, that is to say, that an atom of iron had been an atom of iron since the earth was formed and would so remain to the end of time. The Alchemists were sneered at as fanciful dreamers or madmen, but since Professor J. J. Thomson's discovery [pg 108] of the electron, the atomic theory of matter, is no longer tenable. The principle of radio-activity has later vindicated the Alchemists. Science and the Bible agree in teaching, that all that is, has been formed from one homogeneous substance.

It is that basic principle which John called arche :—primordial matter,—and the dictionary defines Archeology as: "the science of the origin (arche) of things." Masons style God the "Grand Architect," for the Greek word tektos means builder, and God is the Chief Builder (tektos) of arche : the primordial virgin matter which is also the chief source of all things.

Thus we see that when the opening sentence of St. John's gospel is properly translated, our Christian Religion teaches that once a virgin substance enfolded the divine Thinker:—God.

That is the identical condition which the earlier Greeks called Chaos. A little thought will make it evident that we are not arbitrary in finding fault with the translation of the gospel, for it is self-evident that a word cannot be the beginning, a thought must precede the word, and a thinker must originate thought before it can be expressed as a word.

[pg 109]

When properly translated the teaching of John fully embodies that idea, for the Greek term logos means both the reasonable thought,—(we also say Logic),—and the word which expresses this (logical) thought.

1) In the primordial substance was thought, and the thought was with God And God was the word ,

2) that , [The Word], also was with God in the primal state .

Later the divine WORD; the Creative Fiat, reverberates through space and segregates the homogeneous virgin substance into separate forms.

3) Every thing has come into existence because of that prime fact , [The Word of God], and no thing exists apart from that fact.

4) In that was Life.

In the alphabet we have a few elementary sounds from which words may be constructed. They are basic elements of expression, as bricks, iron and lumber are raw materials of architecture, or as a few notes are component parts of music.

But a heap of bricks, iron and lumber, is not a house, neither is a jumbled mass of notes music, nor can we call a haphazard arrangement of alphabetical sounds a word.

[pg 110]

These raw materials are prime necessities in construction of architecture, music, literature or poetry, but the contour of the finished product and the purpose it will serve depends upon the arrangement of the raw materials, which is subject to the constructor's design. Building materials may be formed to prison or palace; notes may be arranged as fanfare or funeral dirge; words may be indited to inspire passion or peace, all according to the will of the designer. So also the majestic rhythm of the Word of God has wrought the primal substance: arche , into the multitudinous forms which comprise the phenomenal world, according to His will.

Did the reader ever stop to consider the wonderful power of a human word. Coming to us in the sweet accents of love, it may lure us from paths of rectitude to shameful ignominy and wreck our life with sorrow and remorse, or it may spur us on in noblest efforts to acquire glory and honor, here or hereafter. According to the inflection of the voice a word may strike terror into the bravest heart or lull a timid child to peaceful slumber. The word of an agitator may rouse the passions of a mob and impel it to awful bloodshed, as in the French Revolution, where dictatorial [pg 111] mandates of mob-rule killed and exiled at pleasure, or, the strain of "Home, Sweet Home" may cement the setting of a family-circle beyond possibility of rupture.

Right words are true and therefore free, they are never bound or fettered by time or space, they go to the farthest corners of the earth, and when the lips that spoke them first have long since mouldered in the grave, other voices take up with unwearying enthusiasm their message of life and love, as for instance the mystical "Come unto me" which has sounded from unnumbered tongues and brought oceans of balm to troubled hearts.

Words of Peace have been victorious,

where war would have meant defeat, and no talent is more to be desired than ability to always say the right word at the auspicious time.

Considering thus the immense power and potency of the human word, we may perhaps dimly apprehend the potential magnitude of the Word of God, the Creative Fiat, when as a mighty dynamic force it first reverberated through space and commenced to form primordial matter into worlds, as sound from a violin bow moulds sand into geometrical figures. Moreover, *the Word of God still sounds* [pg 112] to sustain the marching orbs and impel them onwards in their circle paths, the Creative Word continues to produce forms of gradually increasing efficiency, as media expressing life and consciousness. The harmonious enunciation of consecutive syllables in the Divine Creative Word mark successive stages in evolution of the world and man. When the last syllable has been spoken and the complete word has sounded, we shall have reached perfection as human beings. Then Time will be at an end, and with the last vibration of the Word of God, the worlds will be resolved into their original elements. Our life will then be "hid with Christ in God," till the Cosmic Night:—Chaos,—is over, and we wake to do "greater things" in a "new heaven and a new earth."

According to the general idea Chaos and Cosmos are superlative antitheses of each other. Chaos being regarded as a past condition of confusion and disorder which has long since been entirely superseded by cosmic order which now prevails.

As a matter of fact, Chaos is the seed-ground of Cosmos, the basis of all progress, for thence come all IDEAS which later materialize [pg 113] as Railways, Steamboats, Telephones, etc.

We speak of "thoughts as being conceived by the mind," but as both father and mother are necessary in the generation of a child, so also there must be both *idea* and *mind* before a *thought* can be conceived. As semen germinated in the positive male organ is projected into the negative uterus at conception, so ideas are generated by a positive Human Ego in the spirit-substance of the Region of abstract Thought. This idea is projected upon the receptive mind, and a conception takes place. Then, as the spermatozoic nucleus draws upon the maternal body for material to shape a body appropriate to its individual expression, so does each idea clothe itself in a peculiar form of mindstuff. It is then a thought, as visible to the inner vision of composite man, as a child is to its parent.

Thus we see that ideas are embryonic thoughts, nuclei of spirit-substance from the Region of abstract Thought. Improperly conceived in a diseased mind they become vagaries and delusions, but when gestated in a sound mind and formed into rational thoughts they are the basis of all material, moral and [pg 114] mental progress, and the closer our touch with Chaos, the better will be our Cosmos, for in that realm of abstract realities truth is not obscured by matter, it is self-evident.

Pilate was asked "what is Truth," but no answer is recorded. We are incapable of cognizing truth in the abstract while we live in the phenomenal world, for the inherent nature of matter is illusion and delusion, and we are constantly making allowances and corrections whether we are conscious of the fact or not. The sunbeam which proceeds for 90 millions of miles in a straight line, is refracted or bent as soon as it strikes our dense atmosphere, and according to the angle of its refraction, it *appears* to have one color or another. The straightest stick appears crooked when partly immersed in water, and the truths which are so self-evident in the Higher worlds are likewise obscured, refracted or twisted out of all semblance under the illusory conditions of this material world.

"The truth shall set you free," said Christ, and the more we turn our aspirations from material acquisitiveness and seek to lay up treasure above, the more we aim to rise, the oftener we "get in the spirit," the more readily we "shall know truth" and reach liberation [pg 115] from the fetter of flesh which binds us to a limited environment, and attain to a sphere of greater usefulness.

Study of philosophy and science has a tendency to further perception of truth, and as science has progressed it has gradually receded from its erstwhile crude materialism. The day is not far off when it will be more reverently religious than the church itself. Mathematics is said to be "dry," for it doesn't stir the emotions. When it is taught that "the sum of the angles of a triangle is 180 degrees," the dictum is at once accepted, because its truth is self-evident and no feeling is involved in the matter. But when a doctrine such as the Immaculate Conception is promulgated and our emotions are stirred, bloody war, or heated argument, may result, and still leave the matter in doubt. Pythagoras demanded that his pupils study mathematics, because he knew the elevating effect of raising their minds above the sphere of feeling, where it is subject to delusion, and elevating it towards the Region of abstract Thought which is the prime reality.

In this place we are dealing with worlds in particular, and will therefore defer comment [pg 116] upon the remainder of the first 5 verses of St. John's gospel:

" And Life became Light in man,
5) and Light shines in Darkness. "

We have now seen that the earth is composed of three worlds which interpenetrate one another so that it is perfectly true when Christ said that "heaven is within you" or, the translation should rather have been *among you* . We have also seen that of these three realms two are subdivided. It has also been explained that each division serves a great purpose in the unfoldment of various forms of life which dwell in each of these worlds, and we may note in conclusion, that the lower regions of the Desire World constitute what the Catholic religion calls Purgatory , a place where the evil of a past life is transmuted to good, usable by the spirit as conscience in later lives. The higher regions of the Desire World are the *first Heaven* where all the good a man has done is assimilated by the spirit as *soul* power. The Region of concrete Thought is the *second Heaven*, where, as already said, the spirit prepares its future environment on earth, and the Region of abstract Thought is the *third Heaven*, [pg 117] but as Paul said, it is scarcely lawful to speak about that.

Some will ask: is there then no hell?—No! *The mercy of God* tends as greatly towards the principle of GOOD as *"the inhumanity of man"* towards cruelty, so that he would consign his brother men to flames of hell during eternity for the puerile mistakes committed during a few years, or perhaps for a slight difference in belief. The writer has heard of a minister who wished to impress his "flock" with the reality of an eternity of hell flames, and to demonstrate the fallacy of a heretical notion entertained by some of his parishioners that when sinners come to hell they burn to ashes and that is the end.

He took with him an alcohol lamp and some asbestos into the pulpit and told his audience that God would turn their souls into a substance resembling asbestos. He showed them that though the asbestos were heated red hot it did not decompose into ashes. Fortunately the day of the hell preacher has gone by, and if we believe the Bible which says that "in God we live and move and have our being," we can readily understand that *a lost soul would be an impossibility*, for were one single soul lost, then [pg 118] logically a part of God Himself would be lost. No matter what our color, our race or our creed, we are all equally the children of God and in our various ways we shall obtain satisfaction. Let us therefore rather look to Christ and forget Creed.
Creed or Christ?
No man loves God who hates his kind,
Who tramples on his Brother's heart and soul.
Who seeks to shackle, cloud or fog the mind
By fears of Hell has not perceived our goal.
God-sent are all religions blest;
And Christ, the Way, the Truth and Life,

To give the heavy-laden rest,
And peace from Sorrow, Sin and Strife.
At his request the Universal Spirit came
To all the churches, not to one alone.
On Pentecostal morn a tongue of flame
Round *each* apostle as a halo shone.
Since then, as vultures ravenous with greed,
We oft have battled for an empty name,
And sought by Dogma, Edict, Creed,
To send each other to the flame.
[pg 119]
Is Christ then divided? Was Cephas or Paul
Nailed to the deathly tree?
If not—then why these divisions at all?
Christ's love doth embrace you and me.
His pure sweet love is not confined
By creeds which segregate and raise a wall;
His love enfolds, embraces *Humankind*
No matter what ourselves or Him we call.
Then why not take Him at His word?
Why hold to creeds which tear apart?
But one thing matters, be it heard,
That brother-love fill every heart.
There is but one thing that the world has need to know;
There is but one balm for all our human woe
There is but one way that leads to heaven above;
That way is human sympathy and love.
[pg 120]

Chapter IV. The Constitution of Man

Our chapter head, "the constitution of man," may surprise a reader who has not previously studied the Mystery teachings, or he may imagine that we intend to give an anatomical dissertation, but such is not our intention. We have spoken of the earth upon which we live as being composed of several invisible realms in addition to the world we perceive by means of our senses. We have also spoken of man as being correlated to these various divisions in nature, and a little thought upon the subject will quickly convince us that in order to function upon the various planes of existence described, it is necessary that a man should have a body composed of their substance, or at least have specialized for his own use, some of the material of each of these worlds.

We have said that finer matter, called desire stuff and mind stuff, permeates our atmosphere [pg 121] and the solid earth, even as blood percolates through all parts of our flesh. But that is not a sufficient explanation to account for all facts of life. If that were all, then minerals, which are interpenetrated by the world of thought and the world of desire, would have thoughts and desires as well as man. This is not the case, so something more than mere interpenetration must be requisite to acquire the faculties of thought and feeling.

We know that in order to function in this world, to live as a physical being among other like beings, we must have a physical body all our own, built of the chemical constituents of this visible world. When we lose it at death, it profits us nothing that the world is full of just the very chemicals needed to build such a body. We cannot then specialize them, and therefore we are invisible to all others. Similarly, if we did not possess a special body made of ether, we should be unable to grow and to propagate. That is the case with the mineral. Had we no separate individual desire body, we should be unable to feel desires and emotions, there would be no incentive to move from one place to another. We should then be stationary [pg 122] as plants, and did we not possess a mind, we should be incapable of thought, and act upon impulse and instinct as animals.

Some one may of course object to this last statement, and contend that animals do think. So far as our domesticated animals are concerned that is partially true, but it is not quite in the same way that we think and reason. The difference may perhaps best be understood if we take an illustration from the electrical field. When an electric current *of high voltage* is passed through a coiled copper wire, and another wire is placed in the center of the coils, that wire will become charged with electricity *of a lower voltage* . So also the animal, when brought within the sphere of human thoughts, evolves a mental activity of a lower order.

Paul, in his writings, also mentions *the natural body* and the *spiritual body* while the man himself is a spirit inhabiting those vehicles. We will briefly note the constitution of the various bodies of man invisible to the physical sight but as objective to spiritual sight as the dense body to ordinary vision.

The Vital Body.

That body of ours which is composed of ether is called the "*vital body* " in Western [pg 123] Mystery Schools, for, as we have already seen, ether is the avenue of ingress for vital force from the sun and the field of agencies in nature which promote such vital activities as assimilation, growth and propagation.

This vehicle is an exact counterpart of our visible body, molecule for molecule, and organ for organ, with one exception, which we shall note later. But it is slightly larger, extending about one and one-half inches beyond the periphery of our dense vehicle.

The spleen is the entrance gate of forces which vitalize the body. In the etheric counterpart of that organ solar energy is transmuted to vital fluid of a pale rose color. From thence it spreads all over the nervous system, and after having been used in the body it radiates in streams, much as bristles protrude from a porcupine.

The rays of the sun are transmitted either directly, or reflected by way of the planets and the moon. The rays directly from the sun give spiritual illumination, the rays received by way of the planets produce intelligence, morality, and soul growth, but the rays reflected by way of the moon make for physical growth, as seen in the case of plants which grow differently when planted in the [pg 124] light of the moon from what is the case when they are planted when the moon is dark. There is also a difference in plants sown when the moon is in barren and fruitful signs of the Zodiac.

The solar ray is absorbed by the human spirit which has its seat in the center of the forehead, the stellar ray is absorbed by the brain and spinal cord, and the lunar ray enters our system through the spleen.

The solar, stellar and lunar rays are three-colored, and in the lunar ray which supplies our vital force, the blue beam is the life of The Father, which causes germination, the yellow beam is the life of The Son, which is the active principle in nutrition and growth, and the red beam is the life of the Holy Spirit, which stimulates to action, dissipating the energy stored by the yellow force. This principle is particularly active in generation.

The various kingdoms absorb this life-force differently, according to their constitution. Animals have only 28 pairs of spinal nerves. They are keyed to the lunar month of 28 days and therefore dependent upon a Groupspirit for an infusion of stellar rays necessary to produce consciousness. They [pg 125] are altogether incapable of absorbing the direct ray of the sun.

Man is in a transition stage, he has 31 pairs of spinal nerves which keys him to the solar month, but the nerves in the so-called cauda-equina—literally horsetail—, at the end of our spinal cord, are still too undeveloped to act as avenues for the spiritual ray of the sun. In proportion as we draw our creative force upward by spiritual thought we develop these nerves and awaken dormant faculties of the spirit. But it is dangerous to attempt that development except under guidance of a qualified teacher, and the reader is earnestly warned not to use any method published in books, or sold, for their practice usually leads to dementia. The safe method is never sold for money or any earthly consideration however large or small; it is always freely given as a reward of merit. "Ask and ye shall receive, seek and ye shall find, knock and it shall be opened" , said the Christ. If our life is a prayer for illumination, the search will not be uncertain, nor the knock without response.

When solar energy has been transmuted in the spleen it traverses the whole nervous system of the body glowing with a most [pg 126] beautiful color of a delicate rosy hue. It answers the same purpose as electricity in a telegraph system. We may string wires between cities, erect telegraph stations, install receivers and transmitters. We may even have operators ready at the keys, but until electric fluid is turned into our wires, the telegraph keys will refuse to click. So also in the body, the human spirit is operator, and from the central station of the brain, nerves ramify, go through the whole body to all the different muscles. When this vitalizing fluid of which we are speaking traverses the nervous system, the Ego may send his commands to the muscles and cause them to move but if the vital fluid for any reason does not flow into a certain part of the body such as an arm or a limb, then the spirit is powerless to move that part of the body and we say that it is paralyzed.

When we are in health, we specialize solar energy in such great quantities that we cannot use it all in the body and therefore it radiates through the pores of our skin in straight streams and serves a similar purpose as an exhaust fan. That machine drives the foul air out of a room or building and keeps the atmosphere within pure and sweet. [pg 127] The excessive vital force which radiates from the body drives out poisonous gases, deleterious microbes and effete matter thus tending to preserve a healthy condition. It also prevents armies of disease germs, which swarm about in the atmosphere, from entering; upon the same principle that a fly cannot wing its way into a building through the exhaust fan. Thus it serves a most beneficent purpose even after it has been utilized in our body and is returning to the free state.

It is a curious and most astounding sight when one first observes how, from exposed parts of the body such as hands and face, there suddenly commences to flow a stream of stars, cubes, pyramids and a variety of other geometrical forms. The writer has more than once rubbed his eyes when he first perceived the phenomenon, for it seemed that he must be suffering from hallucinations.

The forms observed are chemical atoms however, which have served their purpose in the body and are expelled through the pores.

When one has eaten a meal, vital fluid is consumed by the body in great quantities, for it is the cement whereby nature's forces build our food into the body. Therefore the radiations are weakest during the period of [pg 128] digestion. If the meal has been heavy, the outflow is very perceptibly diminished, and does not then cleanse our body as thoroughly as when the food has been digested, nor is it as potent in keeping out inimical germs. Therefore one is most liable to catch cold or other disease by overeating, a fault which should be avoided by all who wish to keep in good health.

During ill health the vital body specializes but little solar energy. Then, for a time, the visible body seems to feed upon the vital body as it were, so that the vehicle becomes more transparent and attenuated at the same rate as the visible body exhibits a state of emaciation. The cleansing odic radiations are almost entirely absent during sickness, therefore complications set in so easily.

Though science has not directly observed this vital body of man, it has upon several occasions postulated the existence of such a vehicle as necessary to account for facts in life and the radiations have been observed by a number of scientists at different times and under varying conditions. Blondlot and Charpentier have called them N-rays after the city of Nantes where the radiations were observed by these scientists, others have [pg 129] named them "The Odic fluid". Scientific investigators who have conducted researches into psychic phenomena have even photographed it when it has been extracted through the spleen by materializing spirits. Dr. Hotz for instance obtained two photographs of a materialization through the German medium, Minna-Demmler. On one a cloud of ether is seen oozing out through the left side of the medium, shapeless and without form. The second picture, taken a few moments later, shows the materialized spirit standing at the medium's side. Other photographs obtained by scientists from the Italian medium Eusapio Palladino show a luminous cloud overhanging her left side.

We said in the beginning of this description that the vital body is an exact counterpart of the dense body with one exception: it is of the opposite sex or perhaps we should rather say polarity. As the vital body nourishes the dense vehicle, we may readily understand that blood is its highest visible expression, and also that a positively polarized vital body would generate more blood than a negative one. Woman who is physically negative has a positive vital body, hence she generates a surplus of blood which is relieved by [pg 130] the periodical flow. She is also more prone to tears, which are white bleeding, than man, whose negative vital body does not generate more blood than he can comfortably take care of. Therefore it is not necessary for him to have the outlets which relieve excess of blood in woman.

The Desire Body.

In addition to the visible body and the vital body we also have a body made of desire stuff from which we form our feelings and emotions. This vehicle also impels us to seek sense gratification. But while the two instruments of which we have already spoken, are well organized, the desire body appears to spiritual sight as an ovoid cloud extending from sixteen to twenty inches beyond the physical body. It is above the head and below the feet so that our dense body sits in the center of this egg-shaped cloud as the yolk is in the center of an egg.

The reason for the rudimentary state of this vehicle is, that it has been added to the human constitution more recently than the bodies previously mentioned. Evolution of form may be likened to the manner in which [pg 131] the juices in the snail first condense into flesh and later become a hard shell. When our present visible body first germinated in the spirit, it was a thought-form, but gradually it has become denser and more concrete until it is now a chemical crystallization. The vital body was next emanated by the spirit as a thought-form and is in the third stage of concretion which is etheric. The desire body is a still later acquisition. That also was a thought form at its inception, but has now condensed to desire stuff, and the mind, which we have only recently received, is still but a mere cloudy thought form.

Arms and limbs, ears and eyes are not necessary to use the desire body, for it can glide through space more swiftly than wind without such means of locomotion as we require in this visible world.

When viewed by spiritual sight, it appears that there are in this desire body a number of whirling vortices. We have already explained that it is a characteristic of desire stuff to be in constant motion, and from the main vortex in the region of the liver there is a constant outwelling flow which radiates towards the periphery of this egg-shaped body and returns to the center through a [pg 132] number of other vortices. The desire body exhibits all the colors and shades which we know and a vast number of others which are indescribable in earthly language. Those colors vary in every person according to his characteristics and temperament and they also vary from moment to moment as passing moods, fancies or emotions are experienced by him. There is however in each one a certain basic color dependent upon the ruling star at the moment of his birth. The man in whose horoscope Mars is peculiarly strong usually has a crimson tint in his aura, where Jupiter is the strongest planet the prevailing tint seems to be a bluish tone, and so on with the other planets.

There was a time in the earth's past history when incrustation was not yet complete, and human beings of that time lived upon islands here and there, amid boiling seas. They had not yet evolved eyes or ears, but a little organ: the pineal gland, which anatomists have called the third eye, protruded through the back of the head and was a *localised organ of feeling*, which warned the man when he came too near a volcanic crater and thus enabled him to escape destruction. Since then the cerebral hemispheres have covered [pg 133] the pineal gland, and instead of a single organ of feeling, the whole body inside and out is sensitive to impacts, which of course is a much higher state of development.

In the desire body every particle is sensitive to vibrations similar to those which we call sight, sounds and feelings and every particle is in incessant motion rapidly swirling about so that in the same instant it may be at the top and bottom of the desire body and impart at all points to all the other particles a sensation of that which it has experienced thus every particle of desire stuff in this vehicle of ours will instantly feel any sensation experienced by any single particle. Therefore the desire body is of an exceedingly sensitive nature, capable of most intense feelings and emotions.

The Mind.

This is the latest acquisition of the human spirit, and in most people who have not yet accustomed themselves to orderly, consecutive thought, it is a mere inchoate cloud disposed particularly in the region of the head. When looking at a person clairvoyantly there appears to be an empty space in the center of the forehead just above and between the [pg 134] eyebrows. It looks like the blue part of a gas flame. That is mind stuff which veils the human spirit, or Ego, and the writer has been told that not even the most gifted seer can penetrate that veil which is said to have been spoken of in ancient Egypt as "the veil of Isis" which none may lift and live, for behind that veil is the Holy of Holies, the temple of our body, where the spirit is to be left secure from all intrusion.

To those who have not previously studied the deeper philosophies the question may occur: But why all these divisions; even the Bible speaks only of soul and body, for most people believe soul and spirit to be synonymous terms. We can only answer that this division is not arbitrary but necessary, and founded upon facts in nature. Neither is it correct to regard the soul and the spirit as synonymous. Paul himself speaks of the natural body which is composed of physical substances: solids, liquids, gases and ethers; he mentions a spiritual body, which is the vehicle of the spirit composed of the mind and desire body, and the spirit itself, which is called Ego in Latin or "I" in English.

That term "I" is an appelation which can only be made by the human spirit of itself. [pg 135] We may all call a dog, dog; or we may call a table, table, and any one else may apply the same name to the dog and to the table, but only a human being can be called "I" and only he himself can apply that most exclusive of all words, I, for this is the badge of self-consciousness, the recognition by the human spirit of *itself* as an entity, separate and apart from all others.

Thus we see that the constitution of man is more complex than appears upon the surface, and we will now proceed to note the effect upon this multiplex being of various conditions of life. [pg 136]

Chapter V. Life and Death

Invisible Helpers and Mediums.

There are two classes of people in the world. In one class the vital and dense bodies are so firmly cemented that the ethers cannot be extracted under any circumstances but remain with the dense body at all times and under all conditions from birth to death. Those people are insensible to any supersensuous sights or sounds. They are therefore usually exceedingly sceptic, and believe nothing exists but what *they* can see.

There is another class of people in whom the connection between the dense and the vital bodies is more or less loose, so that the ether of their vital bodies vibrates at a higher rate than in the first class mentioned. These people are therefore more or less sensitive to the spiritual world.

This class of sensitives may again be divided. Some are weak characters, dominated [pg 137] by the will of others in a *negative* manner, as mediums, who are the prey of disembodied spirits desirous of obtaining a physical body when they have lost their own by death.

The other class of sensitives are strong *positive* characters, who act only from within, according to their own will. They may develop into trained clairvoyants, and be their own masters instead of slaves of a disembodied spirit. In some sensitives of both classes it is possible to extract part of the ether which forms the vital body. When a disembodied spirit obtains a subject of that nature, it develops the sensitive as *a materializing medium*. The man who is capable of extracting his own vital body by an act of will, becomes a citizen of two worlds, independent and free. Such are usually known as Invisible Helpers. There are certain other abnormal conditions where the vital body and the dense body are separated totally or in part, for instance if we place our limb in an uncomfortable position so that circulation of the blood ceases. Then we may see the etheric limb hanging down below the visible limb as a stocking. When we restore circulation and the etheric limb seeks to enter into place, an intense prickly sensation is felt, due to the [pg 138] fact that the little streams of force, which radiate all through the ether, seek to permeate the molecules of the limb and stir them into renewed vibration. When a person is drowning, the vital body also separates from the dense vehicle and the intense prickly pain incident to resuscitation is also due to the cause mentioned.

While we are awake and going about our work in the Physical World, the desire body and mind both permeate the dense and the vital bodies, and there is a constant war between the desire nature and the vital body. The vital body is continually engaged in building up the human organism, while the impulses of the desire body tend to tire and to break down tissue. Gradually, in the course of the day, the vital body loses ground before the onslaughts of the desire body, poisons of decay slowly accumulate and the flow of vital fluid becomes more and more sluggish, until at length it is incapable of moving the muscles. The body then feels heavy and drowsy. At last the vital body collapses, as it were, the little streams of force which permeate each atom seem to shrivel up, and the Ego is forced to abandon its body to the restorative powers of sleep.

[pg 139]
When a building has become dilapidated and is to be *restored* and put in thorough repair, the tenants must move out to let the workmen have a free field. So also when the building of a spirit has become unfit for further use, it must withdraw therefrom. As the desire body caused the damage, it is a logical conclusion that that also must be removed. Every night when our body has become tired, the higher vehicles are withdrawn, only the dense and vital bodies are left upon the bed.

Then the process of restoration commences and lasts for a longer or a shorter time according to circumstances.

At times however, the grip of the desire body upon our denser vehicles is so strong that it refuses to let go. When it has become so interested in the proceedings of the day, it continues to ruminate over them after the collapse of the physical body, and is perhaps only half extracted from that vehicle. Then it may transmit sights and sounds of the desire world to the brain. But as the connections are necessarily askew under such conditions, the most confused dreams result. Furthermore, as the desire body compels motion, the body is very apt to toss about when [pg 140] the desire body is not fully extracted, hence the restless sleep which usually accompanies dreams of a confused nature.

There are times of course when dreams are prophetic and come true, but such dreams result only *after* complete extraction of the desire body, under circumstances where the spirit has seen some danger perhaps, which may befall, and then impresses the fact upon the brain *at the moment of awakening* .

It also happens that the spirit goes upon a soul flight and omits to perform its part of the work of restoration, then the body will not be fit to re-enter in the morning, so it sleeps on. The spirit may thus roam afield for a number of days, or even weeks, before it again enters its physical body and assumes the normal routine of alternating waking and sleep. This condition is called trance , and the spirit may remember upon its return what it has seen and heard in the super-physical realm, or it may have forgotten, according to the stage of its development and the depth of the trance condition. When the trance is very light, the spirit is usually present in the room where its body lies all the time, and upon its return to the body it will be able to recount to relatives all they [pg 141] said and did while its body lay unconscious. Where the trance is deeper, the returning spirit will usually be unconscious of what happened around its body, but may recount experiences from the invisible world.

A few years ago a little girl by the name of Florence Bennett in Kankakee, Illinois, fell into such a trance. She returned to the body every few days, but stayed within only a few hours each time, and the whole trance lasted three weeks, more or less. During the returns to her body she told relatives that in her absence she seemed to be in a place inhabited by all the people who died. But she stated that none of them spoke about dying and no one among them seemed to realize that they were dead. Among those she had seen was a locomotive engineer who had been accidentally killed. His body was mangled in the accident which caused death. The little girl perceived him there walking about minus arms, and with lesions upon his head, all of which is in line with facts usually seen by mystic investigators. Persons who have been hurt in accidents go about thus, until they learn that a mere wish to have their body made whole will supply a new arm or [pg 142] limb, for desire stuff is most quickly and readily molded by thought.

Death.

After a longer or shorter time there comes in each life a point where the experiences which a spirit can gain from its present environment have been exhausted, and life terminates in death.

Death may be sudden and seemingly unexpected, as for instance by earthquake, upon the battle-field, or by accident, as we call it, but in reality, death is never accidental or unforeseen by Higher Powers. Not a sparrow falls to the ground without divine Will. There are along life's path partings of the way, as it were; on one side the main line of life continues onward, the other path leads into what we might call a blind alley. If the man takes that path, it soon ends in death. We are here in life for the sake of gaining experience and each life has a certain harvest to reap. If we order our life in such a manner that we gain the knowledge it is intended we should acquire, we continue in life, and opportunities of different kinds constantly come our way. But if we neglect them, and the life goes into paths which are not congruous [pg 143] to our individual development it would be a waste of time to let us stay in such environment. Therefore the Great and Wise Beings, Who are behind the scene of evolution, terminate our life, that we may have a fresh start in a different sphere of influence. The law of conservation of energy is not confined to the Physical World, but operates in the spiritual realms also. There is nothing in life that has not its purpose. We do wrong to rail against circumstances, no matter how disagreeable, we should rather endeavor to learn the lessons which are contained therein, that we may live a long and useful life. Some one may object, and say: You are inconsistent in your teachings. You say there is really no death, that we go into a brighter existence, and that we have to learn other lessons there in a different sphere of usefulness! Why then aim to live a long life here?

It is very true that we make these claims, and they are perfectly consistent with the other assertions just mentioned, but there are lessons to be learned *here* which cannot be learned in the other worlds, and we have to bring up this physical body through the useless years of childhood, through hot and [pg 144] impulsive youth, to the ripeness of manhood or womanhood, before it becomes of true spiritual use. The longer we live after maturity has been attained, when we have commenced to look upon the serious side of life and started to truly learn lessons which make for soul-growth, the more experience we shall gather and the richer our harvest will be. Then, in a later existence, we shall be so much more advanced, and capable of taking up tasks that would be impossible with less length of life and breadth of activity. Besides, it is hard to die for the man in the prime of life with a wife and growing family whom he loves; with ambitions of greatness unfulfilled; with hosts of friends about him, and with interests all centered upon the material plane of existence. It is sad for the woman whose heart is bound up in home and the little ones she has reared, to leave them, perhaps without anyone to care for them; to know that they have to fight their way alone through the early years when her tender care is needed, and perhaps to see those little ones abused, and she unable to lift a hand, though her heart may bleed as freely as it would in earth life. All these things are sad, and *they bind the spirit to earth* for a much longer [pg 145] time than ordinarily, they hinder it from reaping the experiences it should reap upon the other side of death, and they make it desirable along with other reasons already mentioned to live a long life before passing onwards.

The difference between those who pass out at a ripe old age, and one who leaves this earth in the prime of life, may be illustrated by the manner in which the seed clings to a fruit in an unripe state. A great deal of force is necessary to tear the stone from a green peach; it has such a tenacious hold upon the fruit that shreds of pulp adhere to it when forcibly removed, so also the spirit clings to the flesh in middle life and a certain part of its material interest remain and bind it to earth after death. On the other hand, when a life has been lived to the full, when the spirit has had time to realize its ambitions or to find out their futility, when the duties of life have been performed and satisfaction rests upon the brow of an aged man or woman; or when the life has been misspent and the pangs of conscience have worked upon the man and shown him his mistakes; when, in fact, the spirit has learned the lessons of life, as it must have to come [pg 146] to old age; then it may be likened to the seed of the ripe fruit which falls out clean, without a vestige of flesh clinging thereto, at the moment the encasing pulp is opened. Therefore we say, as before, that though there is a brighter existence in store for those who have lived well, it is nevertheless best to live a long life and to live it to the fullest extent possible.

We also maintain, that no matter what may be the circumstances of a man's death, it is not accidental; it has either been brought about by his own neglect to embrace opportunities of growth, or else life has been lived to the ultimate possible. There is one exception to that rule, and that is due to man's exercise of his divine prerogative of interference. If we lived according to schedule, if we all assimilated the experiences designed for our growth by the Creative Powers, we should live to the ultimate length, but *we ourselves* usually shorten our lives by not taking advantage of opportunities, and it also happens that *other men* may shorten our lives and cut them off as suddenly as the so-called accident whereby the divine rulers terminate our life here. In other words, murder, or fatal accidents brought about *by human [pg 147] carelessness*, are in reality the only termination to life not planned by invisible leaders of humanity. No one is ever compelled to do murder or other evil, or there could not come to them a just retribution for their acts. The Christ said that evil must come but woe unto him by whom it cometh , and to harmonize that with the law of divine justice: "as a man soweth, so shall he also reap," *there must at least be absolute free will in respect to evil acts* .

There are also cases where a person lives such a full and good life of such vast benefit to humanity and to himself, that his days are lengthened beyond the ultimate, as they are shortened by neglect, but such cases are of course too few to allow of their being dwelt upon at length.

Where death is not sudden as in the case of accidents, but occurs at home after an illness, quietly and peacefully, dying persons usually experience a falling upon them as of a pall of great darkness shortly before termination of life. Many pass out from the body under that condition, and do not see the light again until they have entered the superphysical realms. There are many other cases however, where the darkness lifts before the [pg 148] final release from the body. Then the dying person views both worlds at once, and is cognizant of the presence of both dead and living friends. Under such circumstances it very often happens that a mother sees some of her children who have gone before, and she will exclaim joyously: Oh, there is Johnny standing at the foot of my bed; my but hasn't he grown! The living relatives may feel shocked and uneasy, thinking the mother suffering from hallucinations, while in reality she is more clear-sighted than they; she perceives those who have passed beyond the veil who have come to greet and help her to make herself at home in the new world she is entering.

Each human being is an individual, separate and apart from all others, and as experiences in the life of each differ from those of all others in the interval from the cradle to the grave, so we may also reasonably infer that the experiences of each spirit vary from those of every other spirit when it passes through the gates of birth and death. We print what purports to be a spirit message communicated by the late Professor James of Harvard at the Boston spirit temple, and in which he describes sensations which he felt [pg 149] when passing through the gate of death. We do not vouch for its authenticity as we have not investigated the matter personally.

Professor James had promised to communicate after death with his friends in this life, and the whole world of psychic research was and still is on watch for a word from him. Several mediums have claimed that Professor James has communicated through them, but the most remarkable are those given through the Boston spirit temple as follows:

" And this is death, only to fall asleep, only to awaken in the morning and to know that all is well. I am not dead, only arisen.

" I only know that I experienced a great shock through my entire system, as if some mighty bond had been rent asunder. For a moment I was dazed and lost consciousness. When I awakened I found myself standing beside the old body which had served me faithfully and well. To say that I was surprised would only inadequately express the sensation that thrilled my very being, and I realized that some wonderful change had taken place. Suddenly I became conscious that my body was surrounded by many of my friends, and an uncontrollable desire took possession of me to speak and touch them that they might know that I still lived. Drawing a little nearer to that which was so like [pg 150] and yet unlike myself, I stretched forth my hand and touched them, but they heeded me not. "

" Then it was that the full significance of the great change that had taken place flashed upon my newly awakened senses; then it was that I realized that an impenetrable barrier separated me from my loved ones on earth, and that this great change which had taken place was indeed death. A sense of weariness and longing for rest took possession of me. I seemed to be transported through space, and I lost consciousness, to awaken in a land so different and yet so similar to the one which I had lately left. It was not possible for me to describe my sensations when I again regained consciousness and realized that, though dead, I was still alive.

" When I first became conscious of my new environment I was resting in a beautiful grove, and was realizing as never before what it was to be at peace with myself and all the world. "

" I know that only with the greatest difficulty shall I be enabled to express to you my sensations when I fully realized that I had awakened to a new life. All was still, no sound broke the silence. Darkness had surrounded me. In fact, I seemed to be enveloped in a heavy mist, beyond which my gaze could not penetrate. Soon in the distance I discerned a faint glimmer of light, which slowly approached me, and then, to my wonder and joy, I beheld the face of her who had been my guiding star in the early days of my earth life. "
[pg 151]

One of the saddest sights witnessed by the seer at a death-bed is the tortures to which we often subject our dying friends on account of ignorance of how to care for them in that condition. We have a science of birth; obstetricians who have been trained for years in their profession and have developed a wonderful skill, assist the little stranger into this world. We have also trained nurses attendant upon mother and child, the ingenuity of brilliant minds is focused upon the problem of how to make maternity easier, neither pains nor money are spared in these beneficent efforts for one whom we have never seen, but when the friend of a lifetime, the man who has served his kind well and nobly in profession, state, or church, is to leave the scene of his labors for a new field of activity, when the woman—who has labored to no less good purpose in bringing up a family to take its part in the world's work—has to leave that home and family, when one whom we have loved all our lives is about to bid us the final farewell, we stand by utterly at a loss how to help; perhaps we even do the very things most detrimental to the comfort and welfare of the departing one.
[pg 152]

Probably there is no form of torture more commonly inflicted upon the dying than that which is caused by administering stimulants. Such potions have the effect of drawing a departing spirit into its body with the force of a catapult, to remain and to suffer for sometime longer. Investigators of conditions beyond have heard many complaints of such treatment. When it is seen that death must inevitably ensue, let not selfish desire to keep a departing spirit a little longer prompt us to inflict such tortures upon it. The death chamber should be a place of the utmost quiet, a place of peace and of prayer, for at that time, and *for three and one-half days after the last breath*, the spirit is passing through a Gethsemane and needs all the assistance that can be given. The value of the life that has just been passed depends greatly upon conditions which then prevail about the body; yes even the conditions of its future life are influenced by our attitude during that time, so that if ever we were our brother's keeper in life, we are a thousand times more so at death.

Post-mortem examinations, embalming and cremation during the period mentioned, not only disturb the passing spirit mentally, but [pg 153] are productive of a certain amount of pain, for there is still a slight connection with the discarded vehicle. If sanitary laws require us to prevent decomposition while thus keeping the body for cremation, it may be packed in ice till the three and one-half days have passed. After that time the spirit will not suffer, no matter what happens to the body.

The Panorama of a Past Life.

No matter how long we may keep the spirit from passing out however, at last there will come a time when no stimulant can hold it and the last breath is drawn. Then the silver cord, of which the Bible speaks, and which holds the higher and the lower vehicles together, snaps in the heart and causes that organ to stop. That rupture releases the vital body, and that with the desire body and mind float above the visible body for from one to three and one-half days while the spirit is engaged in reviewing the past life, an exceedingly important part of its post-mortem experience. Upon that review depends its whole existence from death to a new birth.

The question may arise in the student's mind: How can we review our past life from [pg 154] the cradle to the grave when we do not even remember what we did a month ago, and to form a proper basis for our future life, this record ought to be very accurate, but even the best memory is faulty? When we understand the difference between the conscious and sub-conscious memory and the manner in which the latter operates, the difficulty vanishes. This difference and the manner in which the sub-conscious memory keeps an accurate record of our life experiences may be best understood by an illustration, as follows: When we go into a field and view the surrounding landscape, vibrations in the ether carry to us a picture of everything within the range of our vision. It is as sad as it is true however, that "we have eyes and see not," as the Savior said. These vibrations impinge upon the retina of our eyes, even to the very smallest details, but they usually do not penetrate to our consciousness, and therefore are not remembered. Even the most powerful impressions fade in course of time so that we cannot call them back at will when they are stored in our conscious memory.

When a photographer goes afield *with his camera* the results which he obtains are different. [pg 155] The ether vibrations emanating from all things upon which his camera is focused, transmit to the sensitive plate an impression of the landscape true to the minutest detail, and, mark this well, this true and accurate picture is in no wise dependent upon whether the photographer is observant or not. It will remain upon the plate and may be reproduced under proper conditions. Such is the subconscious memory, and it is generated automatically by each of us during every moment of time, independently of our volition, in the following manner.

From the first breath which we draw after birth to our last dying gasp, we inspire air which is charged with pictures of our surroundings, and the same ether which carries that picture to the retina of our eye, is inhaled into our lungs where it enters the blood. Thus it reaches the heart in due time. In the left ventricle of that organ, near the apex, there is one little atom which is particularly sensitized, and which remains in the body all through life. It differs in this respect from all other atoms which come and go, for it is the particular property of God, and of a certain spirit. This atom may be called the book of the Recording Angel, for [pg 156] as the blood passes through the heart, cycle after cycle, the pictures of our good and evil acts are inscribed thereon to the minutest detail. This record may be called the sub-conscious memory. It forms the basis of our future life when reproduced as a panorama just subsequent to death. By removal of the seed atom—which corresponds to the sensitized plate in a camera,—the reflecting ether of the vital body serves as a focus, and as the life unrolls slowly backwards from death to birth the pictures thereof are etched into the desire body which will be our vehicle during our sojourn in purgatory and the first heaven where evil is eradicated and good assimilated, so that in a future life the former may serve as *conscience* to withhold the man from repeating mistakes of the past, and the latter will spur us to greater good.

A phenomenon similar to the panorama of life usually takes place when a person is drowning. People who have been resuscitated speak of having seen their whole life *in a flash* . That is because under such conditions the vital body also leaves the dense body. Of course there is no rupture of the silver cord, or life could not be restored. Unconsciousness follows quickly in drowning, [pg 157] while in the usual post-mortem review the consciousness continues until the vital body collapses in the same manner that it does when we go to sleep. Then consciousness ceases for a while and the panorama is terminated. Therefore also the time occupied by the panorama varies with different persons, according to whether the vital body was strong and healthy, or had become thin and emaciated by protracted illness. The longer the time spent in review, and the more quiet and peaceful the surroundings, the deeper will be the etching which is made in the desire body. As already said, that has a most important and far reaching effect, for then the sufferings which the spirit will realize in purgatory on account of bad habits and misdeeds will be much more keen than if there is only a slight impression, and in a future life the still small voice of conscience will warn so much more insistently against mistakes which caused sufferings in the past.

When conditions are such at the time of death that the spirit is disturbed by outside conditions, for instance the din and turmoil of a battle, the harrowing conditions of an accident or the hysterical wailings of relatives, the distraction prevents it from realizing [pg 158] an appropriate depth in the etching upon the desire body. Consequently its postmortem existence becomes vague and insipid, the spirit does not harvest fruits of experience as it should have done had it passed out of the body in peace and under normal conditions. It would therefore lack incentive to good in a future life, and miss the warning against evil which a deep etching of the panorama of life would have given. Thus its growth would be retarded in a very marked degree, but the beneficent powers in charge of evolution take certain steps to compensate for our ignorant treatment of the dying and other untoward circumstances mentioned. What these steps are, we shall discuss when considering the life of children in heaven, for the present let it be sufficient to say that in God's kingdom every evil is always transmuted to a greater good though the process may not be at once apparent.

Purgatory.

During life the collapse of the vital body at night terminates our view of the world about us, and causes us to lose ourselves in unconsciousness of sleep. When the vital [pg 159] body collapses just subsequent to death, and the panorama of life is terminated, we also lose consciousness for a time which varies according to the individual. A darkness seems to fall upon the spirit, then after a while it wakes up and begins dimly to perceive the light of the other world, but is only gradually accustomed to the altered conditions. It is an experience similar to that which we have when coming out of a darkened room into sunlight, which blinds us by its brilliancy, until the pupils of our eyes have contracted so that they admit a quantity of light bearable to our organism.

If under such a condition we turn momentarily from the bright sunlight and look back into the darkened room, objects there will be much more plain to our vision than things outside which are illumined by the powerful rays of the sun. So it is also with the spirit, when it has first been released from the body it perceives sights, scenes and sounds of the material world, which it has just left, much more readily than it observes the sights of the world it is entering. Wordsworth in his Ode to Immortality noted a similar condition in the case of new-born children, who are all clairvoyant and much more awake to the [pg 160] spiritual world than to this present plane of existence. Some lose the spiritual sight very early, others retain it for a number of years and a few keep it all through life, but as the birth of a child is a death in the spiritual world and it retains the spiritual sight for a time, so also death here is a birth upon the spiritual plane, and the newly dead retain a consciousness of this world for some time subsequent to demise.

When one awakes in the Desire World after having passed through aforementioned experiences, the general feeling seems to be one of relief from a heavy burden, a feeling perhaps akin to that of a diver encased in a heavy rubber suit, a weighty brass helmet upon his head, leaden soles under his feet and heavy weights of lead upon his breast and back, confined in his operations on the bottom of the ocean by a short length of air tube, and able only to move clumsily with difficulty. When after the day's work such a man is hauled to the surface, and divests himself of his heavy garments and he moves about with the facility we enjoy here, he must surely experience a feeling of great relief. Something like that is felt by the spirit when it has been divested of the mortal coil, and is [pg 161] able to roam all over the globe instead of being confined to the narrow environment which bound it upon earth.

There is also a feeling of relief for those who have been ill. Sickness, such as we know it, does not exist there. Neither is it necessary to seek food and shelter, for in that world there is neither heat nor cold. Nevertheless, there are many in the purgatorial regions who go to all bothers of housekeeping, eating and drinking just as we do here. George Du Maurier in his novel "Peter Ibbetson" gives a very good idea of this condition in the life lived between the hero and the Countess of Towers. This novel also illustrates splendidly what has been said of the sub-conscious memory, for Geo. Du Maurier has somewhere, somehow discovered an easy method which anyone may apply to do what he calls "dreaming true." By taking a certain position in going to sleep, it is possible, after a little practice, to compel the appearance, in a dream, of any scene *in our past life* which we desire to live over again. The book is well worth reading on that account.

When a fiery nebula has been formed in the sky and commences to revolve, a little matter in the center where motion is slowest [pg 162] commences to crystallize. When it has reached a certain density it is caught in the swirl, and whirled nearer and nearer to the outward extremity of what has, by that time, become the equator of a revolving globe. Then it is hurled into space and discarded from the economy of the revolving sun.

This process is not accomplished automatically as scientists would have us believe,—an assertion which has been proven in The Rosicrucian Cosmo Conception and other places in our literature. Herbert Spencer also rejected the nebular theory because it required a First Cause, which he denied, though unable to form a better hypothesis of the formation of solar systems,—but it is accomplished through the activity of a Great Spirit, which we may call God or by any other name we choose. As above, so below, says the Hermetic axiom. Man, who is a lesser spirit, also gathers about himself spirit-substance, which crystallizes into matter and becomes the visible body which the spiritual sight reveals as placed inside an aura of finer vehicles. The latter are in constant motion. When the dense body is born as a child it is extremely soft and flexible.
[pg 163]

Childhood, youth, maturity and old age are but so many different stages of crystallization, which goes on until at last a point is reached where the spirit can no longer move the hardened body and it is thrown out from the spirit as the planet is expelled from the sun. That is death!—the commencement of a disrobing process which continues in purgatory. The low evil passions and desires we cultivated during life have crystallized the desire stuff in such a manner that that also must be expelled. Thus the spirit is purged of evil under the same law that a sun is purged of the matter which later forms a planet. If the life lived has been a reasonably decent one, the process of purgation will not be very strenuous nor will the evil desires thus expurgated persist for a long time after having been freed, but they quickly disintegrate. If, on the other hand, an extremely vile life has been led, the part of the expurgated desire nature may persist even to the time when the spirit returns to a new birth for further experience. It will then be attracted to him and haunt him as a demon, inciting him to evil deeds which he himself abhors. The story of Dr. Jekyll and Mr. Hyde is not a mere fanciful idea of [pg 164] Robert Louis Stevenson, but is founded upon facts well known to spiritual investigators. Such cases are extremes of course, but they are nevertheless possible and we have unfortunately laws which convert such possibilities to probabilities in the case of a certain class of so-called criminals. We refer to laws which decree capital punishment as penalty of murder.

When a man is dangerous he should of course be restrained, but even apart from the question of the moral right of a community to take the life of anyone— which we deny—society by its very act of retaliatory murder defeats the very end it would serve, for if the vicious murderer is restrained under whatever discipline is necessary in a prison for a number of years until his natural death, he will have forgotten his bitterness against his victim and against society, and when he stands as a free spirit in the Desire World, he may even by prayer have obtained forgiveness and have become a good Christian. He will then go on his way rejoicing, and will in the future life seek to help those whom he hurt here.

When society retaliates and puts him to a violent death shortly after he has committed [pg 165] the crime, he is most likely to feel himself as having been greatly injured, and not without cause. Then such a character will usually seek to "get even" as he calls it, he will go about for a long time inciting others to commit murder and other crimes. Then we have an epidemic of murders in a community, a condition not infrequent.

The regicide in Servia shocked the Western World by wiping out an entire royal house in a most shockingly bloody manner, and the Minister of the Interior was one of the chief conspirators. Later he wrote his memoirs, and therein he writes that whenever the conspirators had tried to win anyone as a recruit, they always succeeded when they burned incense. He did not know why, but simply mentioned it as a curious coincidence. To the mystic investigator the matter is perfectly clear. We have shown the necessity of having a vehicle made of the materials of any world wherein we wish to function. We usually obtain a physical vehicle by going through the womb, or perhaps in a few special cases from a particularly good materializing medium, but where it is only necessary to work upon the brain and influence someone else to act, we need but a vehicle [pg 166] made of such ether as may be obtained from fumes of many different substances. Each kind attracts different classes of spirits, and there is no doubt that the incense burned at meetings where the conspirators were successful was of a low and sensual order and attracted spirits who had a grudge against humanity in general and the King of Servia in particular. These malcontents were unable to injure the King himself, but used a subtle influence which helped the conspirators in their work. The released murderer who has a grudge against society on account of his execution, may enter low gambling saloons where the fumes of liquor and tobacco furnish ample opportunity for working upon the class of people who congregate in such places, and the man whose spiritual sight has been developed is often sadly impressed when he sees the subtle influences to which those who frequent such places are exposed. It is a fact of course that a man must be of a low caliber to be influenced by low thoughts, and that it is as impossible to incite a person of benevolent character to do murder—unless we put him into a hypnotic sleep—as to make a tuning fork which vibrates to C sing by striking another attuned to the key of G, [pg 167] but the thoughts of both living and dead constantly surround us, and no man ever thought out a high spiritual philosophy under the influence of tobacco fumes or while imbibing alcoholic stimulants. Were capital punishment, newspaper notoriety of criminals, the *manufacture* of liquor and tobacco eliminated from society, the gun factories would soon cease to advertise and go out of business along with most of the locksmiths. The police force would decrease, so would jails and taxes would be correspondingly minimized.

When a person enters purgatory he is exactly the same person as before he died. He has just the same appetites, likes and dislikes, sympathies and antipathies, as before. There is one important difference, however, namely, that *he has no dense body wherewith to gratify his appetites* . The drunkard craves drink, in fact, far more than he did in this life, but has no stomach which can contain liquor and cause chemical combustion necessary to bring about the state of intoxication in which he delights. He may and does enter saloons, where he interpolates his body into the body of a physical drunkard, so that he may obtain his desires at second hand as it were, he will incite his victim to drink more [pg 168] and more. Yet there is no true satisfaction. He sees the full glass upon the counter but his spirit hand is unable to lift it. He suffers tortures of Tantalus until in time he realizes the impossibility of gratifying his base desire. Then he is free to go on so far as that vice is concerned. He has been purged from that evil without intervention of an angry deity or a conventional devil with hell's flames and pitchfork to administer punishment, but under the immutable law that as we sow so shall we reap, he has suffered exactly according to his vice. If his craving for drink was of a mild nature, he would scarcely miss the liquor which he cannot there obtain. If his desires were strong and he simply lived for drink, he would suffer veritable tortures of hell without need of actual flames. Thus the pain experienced in eradication of his vice would be exactly commensurate with the energy he had expended upon contracting the habit, as the force wherewith a falling stone strikes the earth is proportionate to the energy expended in hurling it upwards into the air.

Yet it is not the aim of God to "get even;" *love* is higher than *law* and in His wonderful mercy and solicitude for our welfare He has [pg 169] opened the way of repentance and reform whereby we may obtain forgiveness of sin, as taught by the Lord of Love: the Christ. Not indeed contrary to law, for His laws are immutable, but by application of a higher law, whereby we accomplish here that which would otherwise be delayed until death had forced the day of reckoning. The method is as follows:

In our explanation concerning the sub-conscious memory we noted that a record of every act, thought and word is transmitted by air and ether into our lungs, thence to the blood, and finally inscribed upon the tablet of the heart:—a certain little seedatom , which is thus the book of Recording Angels. It was later explained how this panorama of life is etched into the desire body and forms the basis of retribution after death. When we have committed a wrong and our conscience accuses us in consequence, and this accusation is productive of sincere repentance *accompanied by reform* , the picture of that wrong act will gradually fade from the record of our life, so that when we pass out at death it will not stand accusingly against us. We noted that the panorama of life unwinds backwards just after death. Later, in the purgatorial [pg 170] life it again passes before the spiritual vision of the man, who then experiences the exact feeling of those whom he has wronged. He seems to lose his own identity for the time being, and assumes the condition of his one time victim, he experiences all the mental and physical suffering himself which he inflicted upon others. Thus he learns to be merciful instead of cruel, and to do right instead of wrong in a future life. But if he awakens to a thorough realization of a wrong previous to his death, then, as said, the feeling of sorrow for his victim and the restitution or redress which he gives of his own free will, make the suffering after death unnecessary, hence— "his sin is forgiven."

The Rosicrucian Mystery teaching gives a scientific method whereby an aspirant to higher life may purge himself continually, and thus be able to entirely avoid existence in purgatory. Each night after retiring the pupil reviews his life during the past day *in reverse order* . He starts to visualize as clearly as possible the scene which took place just before retiring. He then endeavors to impartially view his actions in that scene examining them to see whether he did right or wrong. If the latter, he endeavors to *feel and realize as* [pg 171] *vividly as possible* that wrong. For instance, if he spoke harshly to someone, and upon later consideration finds it was not merited, he will endeavor to *feel* exactly as that one felt whom he wronged and at the very earliest opportunity to apologize for the hasty expression. Then he will call up the next scene in backward succession which may perhaps be the supper table. In respect of that scene he will examine himself as to whether he ate to live, sparingly and of foods prepared without suffering to other creatures of God, (such as flesh foods that cannot be obtained without taking life). If he finds that he allowed his appetite to run away with him and that he ate gluttonously, he will endeavor to overcome these habits, for to live a clean life we must have a clean body and no one can live to his highest possibilities while making his stomach a graveyard for the decaying corpses of murdered animals. In this respect there occurs to the writer a little poem by Ella Wheeler Wilcox:
" I am the voice of the voiceless;
Through me the dumb shall speak,
Till a deaf world's ear
Shall be made to hear
The wrongs of the wordless weak.
[pg 172]
The same force formed the sparrow
That fashioned man the king;
The God of the whole
Gave a spark of soul
To furred and feathered thing.
And I am my brother's keeper
And I will fight his fight,
And speak the word
For beast and bird
Till the world shall set things right.

Thus the pupil will continue to review each scene *in reverse order* from night till morning, and to *feel really sorry* for whatever he has done amiss. He will not neglect to *feel glad* either when he comes to a scene where he has done well, and *the more intensely he can feel, the more thoroughly he will eradicate the record upon the tablet of the heart and sharpen his conscience* , so that as time goes on from year to year, he will find less cause for blame and enhance his soul power enormously. Thus he will grow in a measure impossible by any less systematic method, and there will be no necessity for his stay in purgatory after death.

This evening exercise and another, for the morning, if persistently performed day by [pg 173] day, will in time awaken the spiritual vision as they improve life. This matter has, however, been so thoroughly treated in number 11 of the lecture series: "Spiritual Sight and Insight; its safe culture and control ," that it is unnecessary to dwell upon the matter further in this place.

The First Heaven.

In the first heaven, which is located in the higher regions of the Desire World, the panorama of life again unrolls and reveals every scene where we aimed to help or benefit others. They were not felt at the time the spirit was in the lower regions, for higher desires cannot express themselves in the coarse matter composing the lower regions of the Desire World, but when the spirit ascends to the first heaven it reaps from each scene all the good which it expressed in life. It will feel the gratitude poured out by those whom it helped; if it comes to a scene where itself received a favor from others *and was grateful* , it will experience the gratitude anew. The sum of all these feelings is there amalgamated into the spirit to serve in a future life as incentives to good.
[pg 174]
Thus, the soul is purged from evil in purgatory, and strengthened in good in the first heaven. In one region the extract of sufferings become *conscience* to deter us from doing wrong, in the other region the quintessence of good is transmuted to *benevolence* and altruism which are the basis of all true progress. Moreover, purgatory is far from being a place of *punishment* , it is perhaps the most beneficent realm in nature, for *because of purgation we are born innocent* life after life. The tendencies to commit the same evil for which we suffered remain with us and temptations to commit the same wrongs will be placed in our path until we have consciously overcome the evil here; temptation is not sin, however, the sin is in yielding.

Among the inhabitants of the invisible world there is one class which lives a particularly painful life, sometimes for a great many years, namely, the suicide who tried to play truant from the school of life. Yet it is not an angry God or a malevolent devil who administers punishment, but an immutable law which proportions the sufferings differently to each individual suicide.

We learned previously, when considering the World of Thought, that each form in this [pg 175] visible world has its archetype there,—a vibrating hollow mold which emits a certain harmonious sound; that sound attracts and forms physical matter into the shape we behold, much in the same manner as when we place a little sand upon a glass plate and rub the edge with a violin bow, the sand is shaped into different geometrical figures which change as the sound changes.

The little atom in the heart is the sample and the center around which the atoms in our body gather. When that is removed at death, the center is lacking, and although the archetype keeps on vibrating until the limit of the life has been reached—as also previously explained,—no matter can be drawn into the hollow shape of the archetype and therefore the suicide feels a dreadful gnawing pain as if he were hollowed out, a torture which can only be likened to the pangs of hunger. In his case, the intense suffering will continue for exactly as many years as he should have lived in the body. At the expiration of that time, the archetype collapses as it does when death comes naturally. Then the pain of the suicide ceases, and he commences his period of purgation as do those who die a natural death. But the memory of sufferings experienced [pg 176] in consequence of the act of suicide will remain with him in future lives and deter him from a similar mistake.

In the first heaven there is a class who have not had any purgatorial existence and who lead a particularly joyous life: the children. Our homes may be saddened almost beyond endurance when the little flower is broken and the sunshine it brought has gone. But could we see the beautiful existence which these little ones lead, and did we understand the great benefits which accrue to a child from its limited stay there, our sorrow would be at least ameliorated in a great measure, and the wound upon our heart would heal more quickly. Besides, as nothing else in the world happens without a cause, so there is also a much deeper cause for infant mortality than we are usually aware of, and as we awake to the facts of the case, we shall be able to avoid in future the sorrow incident to loss of our little ones.

To understand the case properly we must revert to the experiences of the dying in the death hour. We remember that the panorama of the past life is etched upon the desire body during a period varying from a few hours to three and one-half days, just subsequent [pg 177] to demise. We recall also, that upon the depth of this etching depends the clearness of the picture, and that the more vivid this panorama of life, the more intensely will the spirit suffer in purgatory and feel the joys of heaven; also, that the greater the suffering in purgatory the stronger the conscience in the next life.

It was explained how the horrors of death upon the battlefield, in an accident or other untoward circumstances would prevent the spirit from giving all its attention to the panorama of life with the result that there would be a light etching in the desire body, followed by a vague and insipid existence in purgatory and the first heaven. It was also stated that hysterical lamentations in the death chamber would produce the same effect.

A spirit which had thus escaped suffering proportionate to its misdeeds, and which had not experienced the pleasure commensurate with the good it had done, would not in a future life have as well developed a conscience as it ought to have, nor would it be as benevolent as it ought to be, and therefore the life, terminated under conditions over which the spirit had no control, would be partly wasted. The Great Leaders of humanity therefore [pg 178] take steps to counteract such a calamity and prevent an injustice. The spirit is brought to birth, caused to die in childhood, it reenters the Desire World and in the first heaven it is taught the lessons of which it was deprived previously.

As the first heaven is located in the Desire World,—which is the realm of light and color,—where matter is shaped most readily by thought, the little ones are given wonderful toys impossible of construction here. They are taught to play with *colors which work upon their moral character* in exactly the manner each child requires. Anyone who is at all sensitive is affected by the color of his clothing and surroundings. Some colors have a depressing effect, while others inspire us with energy, and others again soothe and comfort us. In the Desire World the effect of colors is much more intense, they are much more potent factors of good and evil there than here, and in this color play, the child imbibes unconsciously the qualities which it did not acquire on account of accident or lamentations of relatives. Often it also falls to the lot of such relatives to care for a child in the invisible world, or perhaps to give it birth and see it die. Thus they receive just retribution [pg 179] for the wrong committed. As wars cease, and man learns to be more careful of life, and also how to care for the dying, infant mortality, which now is so appalling, will decrease.

The Second Heaven.

When both the good and evil of a life has been extracted, the spirit discards its desire body and ascends to the second heaven. The desire body then commences to disintegrate as the physical body and the vital body have done, but it is a peculiarity of desire stuff, that once it has been formed and inspired with life, it persists for a considerable time. Even after that life has fled it lives a semi-conscious, independent life. Sometimes it is drawn by magnetic attraction to relatives of the spirit whose clothing it was, and at spiritualistic seances these shells generally impersonate the departed spirit and deceive its relatives. As the panorama of the past life is etched into the shells they have a memory of incidents in connection with these relatives, which facilitates the deception. But as the intelligence has fled, they are of course unable to give any true counsel, and that accounts [pg 180] for the inane, goody-goody nonsense of which these things deliver themselves.

When passing from the first to the second heaven, the spirit experiences the condition known and described previously as "The Great Silence," where it stands utterly alone conscious only of its divinity. When that silence is broken there floats in upon the spirit celestial harmonies of *the world of tone* where the second heaven is located. It seems then to lave in an ocean of sound and to experience a joy beyond all description and words, as it nears its heavenly home—for this is the first of the truly spiritual realms from which the spirit has been exiled during its earth life and the subsequent post-mortem existence. In the Desire World its work was *corrective*, but in the World of Thought the human spirit becomes one with the nature forces and its *creative* activity begins.

Under the law of causation we reap exactly what we sow, and it would be wrong to place one spirit in an environment where there is a scarcity of the necessities of life, where a scorching sun burns the crop and millions die from famine, or where the raging flood sweeps away primitive habitations not built to withstand its ravages, and to bring another [pg 181] spirit to birth in a land of plenty, with a fertile soil which yields a maximum of increase with a minimum of labor, where the earth is rich in minerals that may be used in industry to facilitate transportation of products of the soil from one point to another. If we were thus placed without action or acquiescence upon our part, there would be no justice, but as our post-mortem existence in purgatory and the first heaven is based upon our moral attitude in this life so our activities in the second heaven are determined by our mental aspirations and they produce our future physical environment, for in the second heaven, the spirit becomes part of the nature forces which work upon the earth and change its climate, flora and fauna. A spirit of an indolent nature, who indulges in day dreams and metaphysical speculations *here*, is not transformed by death respecting its mental attitude any more than regarding its moral propensities. It will dream away time in heaven, glorying in its sights and sounds. Thus it will neglect to work upon its future country and return to a barren and arid land. Spirits, on the other hand, whose material aspirations lead them to desire so-called solid comforts of hearth and home, who aim to [pg 182] promote great industries and whose mind is concerned in trade and commerce, will build in heaven a land that will suit their purpose: fertile, immineralized, with navigable rivers and sheltered harbors. They will return in time to enjoy upon earth the fruits of their labors in the second heaven, as they reap the result of their life upon earth in purgatory and the first heaven.

The Third Heaven.

In the third heaven most people have very little consciousness for reasons explained in connection with the Region of Abstract Thought, for there the third heaven is located. It is therefore more of a place of waiting where the spirit rests between the time when its labors in the second heaven have been completed and the time when it again experiences the desire for rebirth. But from this realm inventors bring down their original ideas; there the philanthropist obtains the clearest vision of how to realize his utopian dreams and the spiritual aspirations of the saintly minded are given renewed impetus.

In time the desires of the spirit for further experiences draws it back to rebirth, and the [pg 183] Great Celestial Beings who are known in the Christian Religion as Recording Angels, assist the spirit to come to birth in the place best suited to give it the experience necessary to further unfold its powers and possibilities.

We have all been here many times and in different families, we have had relations of varying nature with many different people and usually there are several families among whom we may seek re-embodiment to work out our self-generated destiny and reap what we have sown in former life. If there are no special reasons why we should take birth in any particular family among certain friends or foes, the spirit is allowed to choose its own place of birth. Thus it may be said that most of us are in our present places by our own prenatal choice.

In order to assist us in making that choice the Recording Angels call up before the spirit's vision a panorama in general outlines of each of the offered lives. This panorama will show what part of our past debts we are to pay, and what fruits we may be expected to reap in the coming life.

The spirit is left free to choose between the several lives offered. But once a choice has [pg 184] been made no evasion is possible during life. We have free will with regard to the future, but the past "*mature*" destiny we cannot escape, as shown by the incident recorded in The Rosicrucian Cosmo Conception, where the writer warned a well known Los Angeles lecturer that if he left his home upon a certain day, he would be injured by a conveyance, in head, neck, breast and shoulders. The gentleman believed and intended to heed our warning. Nevertheless he went to Sierra Madre to lecture upon the fateful day. He was injured in the places stated by a collision and later explained: "I thought the twenty-eighth was the twenty-ninth."

When the spirit has made its choice, it descends into the second heaven where it is instructed by the Angels and Archangels how to build an archetype of the body which it will later inhabit upon earth. Also here we note the operation of the great law of justice which decrees that we reap what we sow. If our tastes are coarse and sensual, we shall build an archetype which will express these qualities; if we are refined and of aesthetic taste, we shall build an archetype correspondingly refined, but no one can obtain a better body than he can build. Then, as the [pg 185] architect who builds a house in which he afterwards lives, will suffer discomfort if he neglects to properly ventilate it, so also the spirit feels disease in a poorly constructed body, and as the architect learns to avoid mistakes and remedy the short-comings of one house when building another, so also the spirit which suffers from defects in its body, learns in time to build better and better vehicles.

In the Region of Concrete Thought, the spirit also draws to itself materials for a new mind. As a magnet draws iron filings but leaves other substances alone, so also each spirit draws only the kind of mind-stuff which it used in its former life, plus that which it has learned to use in its present post-mortem state. Then it descends into the Desire World where it gathers material for a new desire body such as will express appropriately its moral characteristics, and later it attracts a certain amount of ether which is built into the mold of the archetype constructed in the second heaven and acts as cement between the solids, liquids and gaseous material from the bodies of parents which forms the dense physical body of a child, and in due time the latter is brought to birth.

[pg 186]
Birth and Child Life.

It must not be imagined, however, that when the little body of a child has been born, the process of birth is completed. The dense physical body has had the longest evolution, and as a shoemaker who has worked at his trade for a number of years is more expert than an apprentice and can make better shoes and *quicker* , so also the spirit which has built many physical bodies produces them quickly, but the vital body is a later acquisition of the human being. Therefore we are not so expert in building that vehicle. Consequently it takes longer to construct that from the materials not used up in making the lining of the archetype, and the vital body is not born until the seventh year. Then the period of rapid growth commences. The desire body is a still later addition of composite man, and is not brought to birth until the fourteenth year when the desire nature expresses itself most strongly during so-called "hot" youth, and the mind, which makes man man, does not come to birth until the twenty-first year. In law that age is recognized as the earliest time he is fitted to exercise a franchise.

[pg 187]
This knowledge is of the utmost importance to parents, as a proper understanding of the development which should take place in each of the septenary epochs enables the educator to work intelligently with nature and thus fulfill more thoroughly the trust of a parent than those who are ignorant of the Rosicrucian Mystery Teaching. We shall therefore devote the remaining pages to an elucidation of this matter and of the importance of the knowledge of astrology upon the part of the parent.

The Mystery of Light, Color and Consciousness.

"God is Light," says the Bible, and we are unable to conceive of a grander simile of His Omnipresence, or the mode of His manifestation. Even the greatest telescopes have failed to reach the boundaries of light, though they reveal to us stars millions of miles from the earth, and we may well ask ourselves, as did the Psalmist of old: Whither shall I flee from Thy Presence? If I ascend into heaven Thou art there, If I make my bed in the grave (the Hebrew word sheol means grave and not hell), Thou art there, If I take the wings [pg 188] of morning and dwell in the uttermost parts of the sea, even there shall thy hand lead me.

When, in the dawn of Being, God the Father enunciated The Word , and The Holy Spirit moved upon the sea of homogeneous Virgin Matter , primeval Darkness was turned to Light . That is therefore the prime manifestation of Deity, and a study of the principles of Light will reveal to the mystic intuition a wonderful source of spiritual inspiration. As it would take us too far afield from our subject we shall not enter into an elucidation of that theme here, except so far as to give an elementary idea of how divine Life energizes the human frame and stimulates to action.

Truly, God is ONE and undivided, He enfolds within His Being all that is, as the white light embraces all colors. But He appears three-fold in manifestation, as the white light is refracted in three primary colors: Blue, Yellow and Red. Wherever we see these colors they are emblematical of the Father, Son and Holy Spirit. These three primary rays of divine Life are diffused or radiated through the sun and produce Life , Consciousness and Form upon each of the seven light-bearers, the planets, which are called "the [pg 189] Seven Spirits before the Throne." Their names are: Mercury, Venus, Earth, Mars, Jupiter, Saturn and Uranus. Bode's law proves that Neptune does not belong to our solar system and the reader is referred to "Simplified Scientific Astrology" by the present writer, for mathematical demonstration of this contention.

Each of the seven planets receives the light of the sun in a different measure, according to its proximity to the central orb and the constitution of its atmosphere, and the beings upon each, according to their stage of development, have affinity for some of the solar rays. They absorb the color or colors congruous to them, and reflect the remainder upon the other planets. This reflected ray bears with it an impulse of the nature of the beings with which it has been in contact.

Thus the divine Light and Life comes to each planet, either directly from the sun, or reflected from its six sister planets, and as the summer breeze which has been wafted over blooming fields carries upon its silent invisible wings the blended fragrance of a multitude of flowers, so also the subtle influences from the garden of God bring to us the commingled impulses of all the Spirits and [pg 190] in that varicolored light we live and move and have our being.

The rays which come directly from the sun are productive of spiritual illumination, the reflected rays from other planets make for added consciousness and moral development and the rays reflected by way of the moon give physical growth.

But as each planet can only absorb a certain quantity of one or more colors according to the general stage of evolution there, so each being upon earth: mineral, plant, animal and man can only absorb and thrive upon a certain quantity of the various rays projected upon the earth. The remainder do not affect it or produce sensation, any more than the blind are conscious of light and color which exist everywhere around them. Therefore each being is differently affected by the stellar rays and the science of Astrology a fundamental truth in nature, of enormous benefit in the attainment of spiritual growth.

From a horoscopic figure in mystic script we may learn our own strength and weakness, with the path best suited to our development, or we may see the tendencies of those friends who come to us as children, and what traits [pg 191] are dormant in them. Thus we shall know clearly how to discharge our duty as parents, by repressing evil before it comes to birth and fostering good, so that it may bring forth most abundantly the spiritual potencies of the soul committed to our care.

As we have already said, man returns to earth to reap that which he has sown in previous lives and to sow anew the seeds which make for future experience. The stars are the heavenly time keepers which measure the year, the moon indicates the month when time will be propitious to harvest or to sow.

The child is a mystery to us all, we can only know its propensities as they slowly develop into characteristics, but it is usually too late to check when evil habits have been formed and the youth is upon the downward grade. A horoscope cast for the time of birth in a scientific manner shows the tendencies to good or evil in the child, and if a parent will take time and trouble necessary to study the science of the stars, he or she may do the child intrusted to his or her care an inestimable service by fostering tendencies to good and repressing the evil bent of a child ere it has crystallized into habit. Do not imagine that a superior mathematical knowledge is [pg 192] necessary to erect a horoscope. Many construct a horoscope in such an involved manner, so "fearfully and wonderfully made" that it is unreadable to themselves or others, while a simple figure easy of reading may be constructed by anyone who knows how to add and subtract. This method has been thoroughly elucidated in Simplified Scientific Astrology which is a complete text book, though small and inexpensive, and parents who have the welfare of their children thoroughly at heart should endeavor to learn for themselves, for even though their ability may not compare with that of a professional astrologer, their intimate knowledge of the child and their deep interest will more than compensate for such lack and enable them to see most deeply into the child's character by means of its horoscope.

Education of Children.

Respecting the birth of the various vehicles and the influence which that has upon life, we may say that during the time from birth to the seventh year the lines of growth of the physical body are determined, and as it has been noted that sound is builder both [pg 193] in the great and small, we may well imagine that rhythm must have an enormous influence upon the growing and sensitive little child's organism. The apostle John in the first chapter of his gospel expresses this idea mystically in the beautiful words: "In the beginning was the WORD . and without it was not anything made that was made . and the word became flesh;" the word is a rhythmic sound, which issued from the Creator, reverberated through the universe and marshaled countless millions of atoms into the multiplex variety of shapes and forms which we see about us. The mountain, the mayflower, the mouse and the man are all embodiments of that great Cosmic Word which is still sounding through the universe and which is still building and ever building though unheard by our insensitive ears. But though we do not hear that wonderful celestial sound, we may work upon the little child's body by terrestrial music, and though the nursery rhymes are without sense, they are nevertheless bearers of a wonderful rhythm, and the more a child is taught to say, sing and repeat them, to dance and to march to them, the more music is incorporated into a child's daily life, the stronger [pg 194] and healthier will be its body in future years.

There are two mottoes which apply during this period, one to the child and the other to the parent: Example and Imitation . No creature under heaven is more imitative than a little child, and its conduct in after years will depend largely upon the example set by its parents during its early life. It is no use to tell the child "not to mind," it has no mind wherewith to discriminate, but follows its natural tendency, as water flows down a hill, when it imitates. Therefore it behooves every parent to remember from morning till night that watchful eyes are upon him all the time waiting but for him to act in order to follow his example.

It is of the utmost importance that the child's clothing should be very loose, particularly the clothing of little boys, as chafing garments often produce vices which follow a man through life.

If anyone should attempt to forcibly extract a babe from the protecting womb of its mother, the outrage would result in death, because the babe has not yet arrived at a maturity sufficient to endure impacts of the Physical World. In the three septenary periods which follow birth, the invisible vehicles [pg 195] are still in the womb of mother nature. If we teach a child of tender years to memorize, or to think, or if we arouse its feelings and emotions, we are in fact opening the protecting womb of nature and the results are equally as disastrous in other respects as a forced premature birth. Child prodigies usually become men and women of less than ordinary intelligence. We should not hinder the child from learning or thinking of *his own volition* , but we should not goad them on as parents often do to nourish their own pride.

When the vital body is born at the age of seven a period of growth begins and a new motto, or relation rather, is established between parent and child. This may be expressed in the two words Authority and Discipleship . In this period the child is taught certain lessons which it takes upon faith in the authority of its teachers, whether at home or at school, and as memory is a faculty of the vital body it can now memorize what is learned. It is therefore eminently teachable; particularly because it is unbiased by pre-conceived opinions which prevent most of us from accepting new views. At the end of this second period: from about twelve to fourteen, the vital body has been so far developed [pg 196] that puberty is reached. At the age of fourteen we have the birth of the desire body, which marks the commencement of self-assertion. In earlier years the child regards itself more as belonging to a family and subordinate to the wishes of its parents than after the fourteenth year. The reason is this: In the throat of the fœtus and the young child there is a gland called the thymus gland, which is largest before birth, then gradually diminishes through the years of childhood and finally disappears at ages which vary according to the characteristics of the child. Anatomists have been puzzled as to the function of this organ and have not yet come to any settled conclusion, but it has been suggested that before development of the red marrow bones, the child is not able to manufacture its own blood, and that therefore the thymus gland contains an essence, supplied by the parents, upon which the child may draw during infancy and childhood, till able to manufacture its own blood. That theory is approximately true, and as the family blood flows in the child, it looks upon itself as part of the family and not as an Ego. But the moment it commences to manufacture its own blood, the Ego asserts itself, it is no [pg 197] longer Papa's girl or Mamma's boy, it has an "I" -dentity of its own. Then comes the critical age when parents reap what they have sown. The mind has not yet been born, nothing holds the desire nature in check, and much, very much, depends upon how the child has been taught in earlier years and what example the parents have set. At this point in life self-assertion, the feeling "*I am myself*", is stronger than at any other time and therefore authority should give place to Advice ; the parent should practice the utmost tolerance, for at no time in life is a human being as much in need of sympathy as during the seven years from fourteen to twenty-one when the desire nature is rampant and unchecked.

It is a crime to inflict corporal punishment upon a child at any age. Might is never right, and as the stronger, parents should always have compassion for the weaker. But there is one feature of corporal punishment which makes it particularly dangerous to apply it to the youth: namely, that it wakens the passional nature which is already perhaps beyond the control of a growing boy.

If we whip a dog, we shall soon break its spirit and transform it into a cringing cur, [pg 198] and it is deplorable that some parents seem to regard it as their mission in life to break the spirit of their children with the rule of the rod. If there is one universal lack among the human race which is more apparent than any other, it is lack of will, and as parents we may remedy the evil in a large measure by guiding the wills of our children along such lines as dictated by our own more mature reason, so that we help them to grow a backbone instead of a wishbone with which unfortunately most of us are afflicted. Therefore, never whip a child; when punishment is necessary, correct by withholding favors or withdrawing privileges.

At the twenty-first year the birth of the mind transforms the youth into a man or a woman fully equipped to commence his own life in the school of experience.

Thus we have followed the human spirit around a life cycle from death to birth and maturity, we have seen how immutable law governs his every step and how he is ever encompassed by the loving care of the Great and Glorious Beings who are the ministers of God. The method of his future development will be explained in a later work which will deal with "The Christian Mystic Initiation."

[pg 199]

Mt. Ecclesia

(Transcriber's Note: This chapter is the series of pages which, earlier, the author said "had been transferred" to the back of the book.)

A Description of the Headquarters of the Rosicrucian Fellowship

Work in the physical world requires physical means of accomplishment; therefore a tract of land was bought in 1911 in the town of Oceanside, ninety miles south of Los Angeles, California. Southern California was selected because of the abundance of ether in the atmosphere there, and this spot was found to be particularly favored in that respect.

On this commanding site having a wide view of the great Pacific Ocean, of snow capped mountains and smiling valleys, we began to establish our headquarters in the latter part of 1911. Soon after this we erected a sanctuary, the Pro-Ecclesia, where the Rosicrucian Temple Service is held at appropriate times. The Rose Cross Healing Circle holds its meetings there to help sufferers, and it is the place appointed for the united morning and [pg 200] evening devotions of the workers. In the latter half of 1920 we built an Ecclesia, which is designed to be a Temple of Healing. The building, a beautiful domed structure, is of steel and reinforced concrete. It is twelve sided in shape, corresponding to the twelve signs of the zodiac. At the present writing, January, 1921, the final work upon it is just being completed. The esoteric work of the Fellowship will be carried on here.

We have also built a two-story Administration Building to house the general office, the book department, the correspondence school in Christian Mysticism which links Headquarters with students all over the world, and the editorial offices of our monthly publications, notably the "Rosicrucian Fellowship Magazine—Rays from the Rose Cross ." We have also an astrological department which conducts a correspondence school. Its offices are located on the second floor.

The whole first floor is occupied by a modern printing plant and book bindery required to furnish the immense amount of literature needed in this work. In the book department we publish all the standard works and text books of the Rosicrucian Philosophy written by Max Heindel. We are now in process of publishing in book form his former lessons to students.

[pg 201]

In October, 1920, a Training School was established for the preparation of candidates for the lecture field. It is our intention to thereby maintain a Lecture Bureau, from which we will send our lecturers throughout the country to disseminate the teachings and carry the message of our philosophy to the people to a greater extent than has before been possible.

A Dining Hall with seating capacity for over one hundred people affords ample accommodation for workers, students, and patients. The scientific meatless diet served there preserves or restores health, as required in each case. Furthermore, it improves the vitality and mentality in an astonishing degree. A large dormitory, and a number of cottages and tents provide living quarters for all.

By the liberal use of water and the expenditure of much labor, Mount Ecclesia is gradually being transformed into a luxuriant tropical park. There is a deep spiritual purpose in this attempt to make the visible centre of the new world movement beautiful, for it fosters in the workers a poise and peace which are absolutely essential to the proper performance of their work. Without that they cannot escape being disturbed by the flood of sorrow and trouble which flows into Headquarters from [pg 202] members all over the world; without that they cannot continue to put heart into the letters of help, hope and cheer which continually go out to souls who are groaning under the burden of sickness, but by bathing their souls in the beauty of the surroundings, whether consciously or not, they gain in strength and grow in grace, they become better and better fitted for the Great Work in the Master's Vineyard.

In order to aid those who feel the upward urge, to prepare intelligently and reverently for the unfoldment of their inner latent spiritual powers, the Rosicrucian Fellowship maintains two correspondence courses which furnish instruction to students all over the world. One deals with Astrology, the other with Christian Mysticism.

The Astrology to which we refer is not to be confounded with fortune-telling; it is a phase of the Mystic Religion, as sublime as the stars with which it deals, and to the Mystic they are not dead bodies moving in space in obedience to so-called blind natural law, but they are the embodiments of "The Seven Spirits before the Throne," mighty Star-Angels who use their benevolent influences to [pg 203] guide other less exalted beings, humanity included, upon the path of evolution.

There is a side of the moon which we never see, but that hidden half is as potent a factor in creating the ebb and flow, as the part of the moon which is visible. Similarly, there is an invisible part of man which exerts a powerful influence in life, and as the tides are measured by the motion of sun and moon, so also the eventualities of existence are measured by the circling stars, which may therefore be called "the Clock of Destiny," and knowledge of their import is an immense power, for to the competent Astrologer a horoscope reveals every secret of life.

Thus, when you have given an astrologer the data of your birth, you have given him the key to your innermost soul, and there is no secret that he may not ferret out. This knowledge may be used for good or ill, to help or hurt, according to the nature of the man. Only a friend should be trusted with this key to your soul, and it should never be given to anyone base enough to prostitute a spiritual science for material gain.

To the medical man Astrology is invaluable in diagnosing diseases and prescribing a remedy, for it reveals the hidden cause of all [pg 204] ailments, in a manner that has often perplexed the skeptic and dumbfounded the scoffer.

The opinion of thousands is of great value, but it does not prove anything, for thousands may hold an opposite view; occasionally a single man may be right and the rest of the world wrong, as when Galileo maintained that the earth moves. Today the whole world has been converted to the opinion for which he suffered torture, and we assert that, *as man is a composite being, cures are successful only in proportion as they remedy defects on the physical, moral and mental planes of Being*. We also maintain that results may be obtained more easily at certain times when stellar rays are propitious to healing of a particular disease, or by treatment with remedies previously prepared under auspicious conditions.

If you are a parent the horoscope will aid you to detect the evil latent in your child and teach you how to apply the ounce of prevention. It will show you the good points also, that you may make a better man or woman of the soul entrusted to your care. It will reveal systemic weakness and enable you to guard the health of your child; it will show what [pg 205] talents are there, and how the life may be lived to a maximum of usefulness. Therefore, the message of the marching orbs is so important that you cannot afford to remain ignorant thereof.

In order to aid those who are willing to help themselves we maintain a Correspondence Class in Astrology, but make no mistake, we do not teach fortune-telling; if that is what you are looking for, we have nothing for you.

Our Lessons Are Sermons

They embody the highest moral and spiritual principles, together with the loftiest system of ethics, for Astrology is, to us, a phase of religion; we never look at a horoscope without feeling that we are in a holy presence, face to face with an immortal soul, and our attitude is one of prayer for light to guide that soul aright.

We Do Not Cast Horoscopes

Despite all we can say, many people write enclosing money for horoscopes, forcing us to spend valuable time writing letters of refusal and giving us the trouble of returning their money. Please do not thus annoy us; it will avail you nothing.

[pg 206]

The Course in Christian Mysticism

Christ taught the multitude in *parables*, but explained the *mysteries* to His disciples. *Paul gave milk* to the babes, but *meat* to the strong.

Max Heindel, the founder and leader of the Rosicrucian Fellowship, endeavored to follow in their steps and give to interested and devoted students a *deeper teaching* than that promulgated in public.

For that purpose we conduct a correspondence course in Christian Mysticism. The General Secretary may admit applicants to the preliminary course, but *advancement* in the deeper degrees depends upon merit. It is for those alone who have been *tried*, and found true.

How To Apply for Admission

Anyone who is not engaged in for-

tune-telling or similar methods of commercializing spiritual knowledge will, upon request, receive an application blank from the General Secretary, Rosicrucian Fellowship. When this blank is returned properly filled, he may admit the applicant to instruction in either or both correspondence courses.
[pg 207]
The Cost of the Course

There are no fixed fees; no esoteric instruction is ever put in the balance against coin. At the same time, it cannot be given "*free* ," "*for nothing* ," for those who work to promulgate it must have the necessities of life. Type, paper, machinery and postage also cost money, and *unless you pay your part someone else must pay for you* .

There are a few who cannot contribute, and who need these teachings as much or more than those who may take comfort from financial ease or affluence. If they make their condition known, they will receive as much attention as the largest contributors, but others are expected to contribute for their own good as well as for the good of the work. Remember, a closed hand that does not give cannot receive .
[pg 208]

Index

Abstract Thought, see Thought, World of, Region of Abstract Thought .
Action, incentive to, 158 .
Adepts, pupils of schools of the Greater Mysteries, 10 .
Air, charged with pictures of surroundings, 37 , 155 .
Alchemy, proved by radio-activity, 108 .
Alcohol, results of using, 166 .
Ambassador from sun, 87 .
Ameshaspends, Seven Spirits before the Throne, 87 .
Angels, densest body of, composed of ether, 73 ;
expert builders in ether, 74 ;
family spirits, 80 ;
guardians of propagative force, 74 ;
instruct ego in building archetype, 184 ;
one step beyond human stage, 73 .
Angels, Recording, see Recording angels .
Animals, dependent upon group spirit for infusion of stellar rays, 124 ;
keyed to lunar month, 124 ;
thought processes of, 122 .
Aquarian Age, intellect of, 15 .

Archangels, densest vehicle of, 79 ;
[pg 209]
instruct ego in building archetype, 184 ;
less evolved become group spirits, 81 ;
native of Desire World, 79 ;
race and national spirits, 80 ;
various grades of, 80 ;
work with humanity politically and industrially, 80 .
Arche, primordial matter of, 108 .
Archetypal forces direct archetypes, 103 .
Archetype, duration of, 175 ;
vibratory mold, 175 .
Assimilation, through ether, 123 .
Astrology, estimation of time by, in Desire World, 94 ;
value of, 190 .
Atom, physical, spherical shape of, 9 .
Atom, seed, see Seed atom .
Atoms, chemical, expelled through skin, 127 .
Attitude, mental, results of, 181 .
Benevolence, acquired in First Heaven, 174 .
Bennett, Florence, trance of, 141 .
Black magic, punishment of, 17 .
Blood, charged with pictures of surroundings, 155 ;
relation of, to vital body, 129 .
Blue, in stellar ray, life of the Father, 124 , 188 .
Bode's law and Neptune, 189 .
Body, dense, see Dense body .
desire, see Desire body .
vital, see Vital body .
Brain, absorption of stellar rays through, 124 .
Breath, record of, 37 , 38 .
Capital punishment, menace of, 164 .
Carelessness, power of, to shorten life, 147 .

Causation, law of, attraction of like to like, 48 ;
determines environment, 48 , 180 ;
[pg 210]
flexibility of law of, 52 .

Chaos, (Cosmic night) seed ground of Cosmos, 112 ;
state of orderly segregation, 105 .
Chemical atoms, expelled through skin, 127 .
Chemical ether, assimilation and growth by, 69 ;
seen as blue haze, 65 .
Child, post-mortem experiences of, easily investigated, 51 ;
prodigies, 195 .
Children, clairvoyance of, 160 ;
danger of mental forcing, 195 ;
discipline of, 195 ;
individual blood developed in, 196 ;
imitativeness of, 194 ;
proper clothing of, 194 ;
life of, in First Heaven, 176 ;
understanding of, through astrology, 192 .
Christ, higher laws taught by, 169 ;
rebirth taught by, 46 .
Christianity, the flowering of previous religions, 6 .
Clairvoyance of children, 160 ;
of the dying, 148 ;
varieties of, 136 .
Clairvoyants, separation of vital body of, 137 .
Clairvoyants, trained, positive powers of, 137 .
Colors, emotional effect produced by, 178 .
Colors, primary, symbolize God, 188 .
Community affected by executions, 165 .
Concentration in Desire World, 91 .
Concrete Thought, see Thought, World of, Region of Concrete Thought .
Conditions of life related to past action, 43 .
Conscience, assimilated pictures of past experience, 38 , 156 .
Consequence, law of, see Causation, law of .
[pg 211]
Conservation, law of, and survival of spirit, 35 .
Cord, Silver, see Silver Cord .
Corporal punishment, inadvisability of, 197 .
Cosmic night, see Chaos .
Cosmos, aggregate of systematic order,

105.
Countries, egos work upon, 180.
Creation of Cosmos, 188.
Creative force, develops spinal nerves, 125.

Creative Hierarchies, aid humanity, 6;
guide man's evolution, 5, 52;
safeguard man from materialism, 8.
Criminals, care of, 164;
execution of, a menace, 164.
Crucifixion, the Mystic Death, 12.
Crystallization in man's evolution, 163.
Dead, care of, 152;
inhabit Desire World, 88;
intense activity of, 89.
Death, disrobing process of ego, 163;
foreseen by higher powers, 142;
peaceful, helpfulness of, 147;
premature, ill effects of, 145;
problem of, 27;
provides fresh start, 143.
Debts, binding nature of, 49.
Demmler, Minna, materializations by, 129.

Dense body, chemical constituents of, 57;
crystallized spirit substance, 162;
disease of, due to imperfect archetype, 185;
energized by divine life, 188;
improves as spirit progresses, 5;
quality of, dependent upon ego, 184;
most evolved of man's vehicles, 186.
[pg 212]
Desire, created and guided by thought, 58;
forms impelled into action by, 56.

Desire body, basic individual color of, 132;
born at fourteenth year, 186;
capable of sense perception, 133;
cause dreams, 139;
circulation in currents, 133;
colors of, 132;
destructive action of, 138;
extends beyond dense body, 130;
gives ability to experience desire and emotion 121, 130, 133;
impels motion, 56, 139;
impels to sense gratification, 130;
main vortex, in the liver, 131;
rapid locomotion of, 131;
recent acquisition of, 130;
shape of, ovoid, 130;
shell of, persists after death, 163, 179;
vortices of, 131;
war of, with vital body, 138;
withdrawal of, in sleep, 138.
Desire stuff, constant motion of, 77, 131;
elasticity of, 77;
force combined with matter, 77;
modeled by thought, 142;
permeates atmosphere, 120;
persistence of, 179;
responsiveness to feeling, 77.

Desire World, archangels native to, 79;
dead remain in, varying lengths of time, 78;
difficulty of concentration in, 91;
diversity of tongues in, 83;
[pg 213]
effect of colors in, 178;
ego's corrective work in, 168-170;
estimation of time in, 93;
existence of, makes man's desires possible, 57;
force and matter closely related in, 77;
form blends into sound in, 95;
head only perceptible in some regions of, 79;
large population of, 77;
seasons non-existent in, 93;
second vehicle of earth, 55;
time non-existent in, 92;
universal mode of expression in, 85;
vision pertaining to, 66;
world of color, 68.
Earth composed of three interpenetrating worlds, 55, 116;
structure of dense body, obtained from, 57;
training school of, 6, 43;
worked upon, by the disembodied, 104.
Earth lives, intervals between, 52.
Earth spirits, fairies and elves, 70.
Eastern Wisdom, unsuited to Western peoples, 14.
Ego, see Spirit, threefold.
Egyptians painted group spirits, 82.
Electron, discovery of, 107.
Elves, spirits of mountains, 70.
Emotions, relation of, to desire body, 186.
Enmity overcome by its own discomforts, 49.
Environment, suffering caused by, 49.
Ether, avenue for solar forces, 70, 74, 123;
nature of, 62;
permeates atomic structure of dense matter, 62.
Ether, chemical, see Chemical ether.
Ether, life, see Life ether.
[pg 214]
Ether light, see Light ether.
Ether, reflecting see Reflecting ether.
Etheric sight, distinguished from spiritual, 66;
extension of physical, 65;
penetrates opaque substances, 66;
shows all objects same color, 67.
Ethers, separation of, 136.
Ever-existing essence, 107.
Evil and good acts recorded by breath, 38;
destruction of, 39;
transmutation of, to good, 158.
Evolution, from life to life, 53;
manifests in rest and activity, 42;
of vehicles, manner of, 185;
persistent unfoldment in, 42.
Fairies, spirits of the mountains, 70.
Fate, ripe, unavoidability of, 184.
Faults, correction of, 169.
Feeling, right, increases conscience, 172.
First cause, necessity for, 162.
First hand knowledge, possible to all, 52.

First Heaven, good of past life reaped in, 173;
good strengthened in, 174;
panorama of life in, 173;
upper regions of Desire World, 173.
Fluid, vital, cessation of flow of, 138.
Forgiveness of sin, 164, 169.
Form, archetypes of, 175;
incapable of feeling, 60.
Forms, impelled into action by desire, 56.
Forms, physical, built from chemical substance, 55.
Free will, existence of, 147;
pertaining to future, 184.
[pg 215]
Generation caused by red ray of Holy Spirit, 124.
Germination caused by blue ray of Father, 124.

Gnomes, earth spirits, 70.
God, immanence of, 187.
Good amalgamates with spirit, 39;
and evil acts recorded by breath, 38.

Great Silence between Desire World and World of Thought, 95, 180;
may be entered by acts of will, 96.
Group spirit, brings stellar influence to animals, 124;
less evolved archangels, 81;
painted by Egyptians, 82.
Growth, physical, carried on through ether, 123;
caused by yellow rays of Son, 124;
relation of, to moon, 124;
relation of, to vital body, 186.
Growth, spiritual, must be slow, 103.
Heaven, among you, 116.
Heaven, First, see First Heaven.
Heaven, Second, see Second Heaven.
Heaven, Third, see Third Heaven.
Hell, existence of, impossible, 117.
Helpers, Invisible, see Invisible Helpers.
Heredity, of the physical only, 47.
Hierarchies, Creative, see Creative Hierarchies.
Higher Self dominates lower by keynote, 99.
Higher senses of man, 16.
Higher vehicles, permeability of, 138;
withdrawal of, in sleep, 138.
Holy of Holies, temple of our bodies, 134.
Hotz, Dr., spirit photographs taken by, 129.
Humanity, two classes of, 136.
I, badge of self-consciousness, 135.
[pg 216]
Ideas clothe themselves in mind stuff, 113;
embryonic thoughts, 113;
generated by ego in Region of Abstract Thought, 113;
originate in chaos, 112.
Ignorance, man's one sin, 42.
Illumination, induced by solar rays, 123.
Immaculate conception, the Mystic Birth, 12.
Immortality of spirit, 39.
Incense, evil effects of, 165.
Incentive, induced by etchings of life panorama, 158.

Individual auric color, dependent upon ruling planet, 132.
Infant mortality, causes of, 176-179.
Intelligence induced by planetary rays, 123.
Interval between earth lives, 52.

Invisible Helpers, faculties of, 137;
linguistic abilities, valuable to, 83.
Izzards, 87.
James, Professor William, reputed communication from, 149-151.
Jehovah, see Holy Spirit.
John, Gospel of, spiritual significance of, 105.
Jupiter, auric color of, 132.
Karma, see Causation, law of.
Keynote, creates and maintains form, 98;
manifestation of Higher Self, 99;
stopping of, terminates life, 100;
Voice of Silence, 99.
Knowledge, the only salvation, 42.
Laws of nature, living intelligences, 53.
Life, dualistic theory of, 29;
lengthened by good deeds, 147;
long, value of, 144, 146;
monistic theory of, 29;
[pg 217]
object of, gaining of experience, 142;
shortened by neglected opportunities, 146.

Life ether, propagation accomplished through medium of, 69.

Life panorama, backward unfoldment of, 156;
duration of, 153;
importance of, 153, 158;
insufficient, causes infant mortality, 177;
sub-conscious memory, basis of, 154;
terminated by collapse of vital body, 157.
Light, relation of, to creation, 188.

Light ether, motion due to, 69;
transmits solar force, 69.
Likes and dislikes determine environment, 48.
Liver, main vortex of desire body, 131.
Logos, Reasonable Thought, 109.
Love, higher than law, 168;
supreme commandment, 90.

Lunar ray enters body through spleen, 124.;
induces physical growth, 123, 190.;
three-fold constitution of, 124.
Magic, black, punishment of, 17.
Man, born innocent of sin, 174;
composite being of body, soul, spirit, 36;
desires of, impel to action, 56;
gathers spiritual substance, 162;
Great Beings safeguard, 198;
has evolved from lower forms, 73;
higher vehicles of, 120;
keyed to solar month, 125;
made a little lower than angels, 73;
spinal nerves of undeveloped, 125;
spiritual faculties of, 15.
[pg 218]
Mars, auric color of, 132.
Materialism and spirituality, necessity of, 7.
Materialistic theory of life, 34-36.
Materialization through incense, 165;
through mediums, 129.
Mathematics, benefit derived from study of, 115.
Matter, illusory nature of, 114.
Mediums and negative clairvoyance, 137;
read in reflecting ether, 70.
Memory of Nature, events recorded in, 94.
Memory of past lives, 50.
Memory, sub-conscious, see Sub-conscious memory.
Metamorphosis in higher worlds, 32.
Michael, ambassador from sun to earth, 87.
Michael, archangel, guardian of Jews, 80.
Mind, born at twenty-first year, 186, 198;
cloudy thought form, 131, 133;
material for, acquired in Region of Concrete Thought, 185;
recent acquisition of, 131.

Mind, Lords of, expert builders of mind stuff, 102;
help man to acquire mind, 103;
human during dark stage of earth, 101;
Powers of Darkness, 101;
worked with man in mineral stage, 102.
Mind stuff, permeability of, 120;

veils inner spirit, 134.
Monistic, theory of life, 29.
Moon rays, see Lunar rays.
Morality induced by planetary rays, 123, 190.
Music in Desire World, 68;
soul-speech of World of Thought, 68.

Mystery Orders formed on cosmic lines, 9;
[pg 219]
seven world workers in, 9.
N-rays, etheric radiation of, 128.
Nature, laws of, control nature spirits, 72;
Great Intelligences, 70.
Nebulae, fiery formation of, 161.
Nebular theory postulates First Cause, 162.
Negative development, mediumship allied to, 137.
Nephesh, 37.
Neptune outside of our solar system, 189.
Occult orders, see Mystery orders.
Odic fluid, see Solar fluid.
Opportunities, each life contains, 142.
Over-eating, ill-effects of, 128.
Painting, related to Desire World, 68.
Palladino, Eusapio, materializations through, 129.
Panorama of Life, see Life Panorama.
Patriotism, inspired by archangels, 80.
Periodicity, law of, determines time of actions, 13.
Personality governed by keynote, 99.
"Peter Ibbettson," occult information in, 161.
Physical body, anchor of mind, 92.
Physical embodiment, value of, 90, 143.
Pineal gland, localized organ of feeling, 132;
spiritual sight through development of, 66;
third eye, 132.
Planetary ray, see Stellar ray.

Planetary spirits, color belonging to, 189;
names of, 189.
Planets, absorption of solar rays by, 188.
Post-mortem experiences, usefulness of, 143.

Powers of Darkness, see Mind, Lords of.

Powers, spiritual, difficulty of obtaining, 64;
microscopic and telescopic, 64;
[pg 220]
possible to all, 64.
Prayer, forgiveness of sin through, 164.
Precession of equinoxes, measure of time, 94.
Predestination of great leaders, 45, 46.
Primary colors symbolize God, 188.
Probation, long, necessity for, 64.
Propagation carried on through life ether, 123.
Psychometrists read in reflecting ether, 70.
Puberty, cause of, 196.
Pituitary body and clairvoyance, 66.
Punishment, corporal, evils of, 198.
Purgatory, evil habits corrected in, 167;
evil of past lives transmuted in, 116;
experiences in, based on moral attitude of preceding life, 181;
review of life experiences in, 170.
Race likeness caused by race spirits, 81.
Race Spirits, see Archangels.

Rebirth, law of, alternation of sex in, 52;
believed in, by Jews, 46;
Biblical foundation for doctrine of, 46;
explanation of inequalities, 43, 47;
harmonious with nature's methods, 47;
intervals between, 52;
preparations for, 185;
special talents of individual, evidence of, 46;
specially adapted to ego's need, 52;
taught by Christ, 46.

Recording angels aid ego in choice of environment, 183;
give race religions, 6, 14;
show ego life panorama, 183.
Red in stellar ray, life of Holy Spirit, 124;
produces form, 188.
[pg 221]

Reflecting ether, impressions of universe recorded in, 69;
mediums and psychometrists read in, 70.
Regret, time wasted in, 92.
Reincarnation, see Rebirth.
Religions, all have origin in God, 104.
Repentance, benefits received through, 169.
Restrospection, exercise of, 170-173.
Ripe fate, unavoidability of, 184.
Rose Cross, initiates into science of life and being, 8;
Mystery school of the West, 8;
thirteen Brothers of, 9;
thirteenth member, the invisible head, 9;
works to mould public opinion, 11.
Rosicrucian Fellowship, herald of the Aquarian Age, 15;
purpose and work of, 14-18.
Rosicrucians, hold doctrine of man's potential divinity, 5;
hierophants of Lesser Mysteries, 10;
influence of, upon writers of modern times, 11;
midnight service of, 11;
object of, to unite religion and science, 12;
work with evolved humanity, 9.
Ruling planet, relation of color of, 132.
Salamanders, fire spirits, 71;
produce volcanic eruptions, 72.
"School of Athens," painting of, 29.
Science discovers spiritual side of universe, 34;
established proofs of spirit survival, 35;
spiritualized by Rosicrucians, 11.
Sculpture belongs to physical world., 68.

Second Heaven, ego prepares future environment in, 116;
located in Region of Concrete Thought, 116.

Seed atom, basis of sub-conscious memory, 156;
etchings of, 37;
[pg 222]
sample and center of other dense atoms, 175;
transmits pictures to desire body, 156.
Sensitives, separation of ethers in vital body of, 136.
Servia, regicides in, 165.
Seven Spirits before the Throne, see Planetary Spirits.

Sex, alternation of, 52.
Shells, discarded desire bodies, 179;
retain life panorama, 179;
spiritualistic impersonations by, 179.

Sight, spiritual, accompanies development of pineal gland and pituitary body, 66;
varieties of, 67.
Silence, Great, see Great Silence.
Silence, Voice of, see Voice of the Silence.

Silver cord holds higher and lower vehicles together, 153;
snapping of, 153.

Solar fluid, absorption of, by different kingdoms, 124;
aids in digestion, 127;
cleansing power of, 128;
expels disease germs, 127;
muscular movement by means of, 126;
permeates nervous system, 123, 126;
radiates from body, 123;
transformed to rose color, 123, 126.
Solar rays, direct and indirect, 123;
spiritual illumination from, 123;
three-fold constitution of, 124.
Soul, differentiated from spirit, 134;
product of breath, 37.
Soul flights, time non-existent in, 89.
Soul growth induced by planetary rays, 123.
Soul power, assimilated from past action, 116;
developed by good action, 38.
[pg 223]
Sound, power of, over matter, 175.
Spinal cord, absorbs stellar ray, 124.
Spencer, Herbert, and nebular hypothesis, 162.
Sphinx, faces east, 28;
riddle of, 28.

Spirit, threefold (ego) abandons vital body in sleep, 138;
absorbs solar ray, 124;
destined to become creative intelligence, 103;
disembodied, relief of, at leaving body, 161;
distinguished from soul, 134;
drawn to rebirth by desire for experience, 182;

earth-bound, condition of, 144;
encrusted in mind stuff, 101;
free will of, 184;
freedom of, in choosing environment, 183;
has seat in forehead, 124;
immortality of, 39;
improvement in vehicles of, 185;
individualization of, in childhood, 196;
instructed in building archetype, 184;
many earth lives of, 183;
no limitations possible for, 104;
sowing and reaping of, 104;
sufferings of, in purgatory, 163;
uncreate and eternal, 39;
various human relations of, 183;
works with archetypes, 103, 180.
Spirits, planetary, see Planetary Spirits.
Spiritual investigations, 63.
Spiritual powers, see Powers, spiritual.
Spiritual sight, see Sight, spiritual.
Spiritual thought, spinal nerves developed by, 125.
Spirituality followed by materialism, 7.
[pg 224]
Spleen, entrance for solar forces, 123;
transmutation for solar energy in, 123.

Stellar ray, absorption of, by brain and spinal cord, 124;
animals incapable of absorbing, 124;
induces morality, 123, 190;
threefold nature of, 124.
Stimulants, effects of, upon dying, 152.
Storms caused by nature spirits, 71.

Sub-conscious memory, basis of future life, 156;
consciously utilized, 161;
in seed atom, 155;
retentiveness of, 154.
Suicide, sufferings of, 174.
Sun, movements of, 94.
Superman, evolution of man into, 53.
Survival after death, established by scientists, 35.
Sylphs, spirits of mists, 70.
Tears, white bleeding, 130.
Temptation, repetition of, 174.
Theological theory of life, 36-39.

Third Heaven, few have consciousness in, 182;
in Region of Abstract Thought, 116, 182;

inspiration of philanthropist, 182;
place of awaiting rebirth, 182;
source of inventor's inspiration, 182.
Thompson, J. J., discovery of electron by, 107.
Thought, objects of physical world, crystallized, 97, 131;
result of union, idea and mind stuff, 113.

Thought, world of, earth's finest vehicle, 55;
home of spirit, 58;
knowledge gained in, 100;
makes man's thought possible, 57;
realm of tone, 180;
[pg 225]
spirit's work in, 180;
time non-existent in, 101;
tonal vision pertaining to, 67.

Thought, World of, Region of Abstract Thought, abstract verities of, 106;
Third Heaven in, 116.

Thought, World of, Region of Concrete Thought, acme of reality, 97;
mind built in, 185;
physical world replica of, 97;
Second Heaven, 116.
Thymus Gland, function of, 196.
Time, end of, 112;
relatively non-existent in higher worlds, 92.
Tobacco, fumes of, disembodied work through, 166.
Trance, caused by flight of spirit, 140;
kinds of, 140.
Truth, freedom by, 114;
self-evident in higher worlds, 114.
Undines, spirits of water, 70.
Vehicles, improvements in, 185.
Veil of Isis, 134.
Vibration, external, transferred to blood, 37;
universality of, 36.

Vital body, born at seventh year, 195;
collapse of, in sleep, 138;
composed of ether, 122;
connected with spleen, 123;
disintegration of, stops life panorama, 157;
extends beyond dense vehicle, 123;
in sickness lacks solar rays, 128;

in third stage of evolution, 131 ;
nourishes dense body, 129 ;
[pg 226]
photographed by scientists, 129 ;
polarity of, 129 ;
propagation by, 121 ;
recuperative work of, 138 ;
second vehicle acquired by man, 186 ;
separation of ethers of, 137 ;
war with desire body, 138 ;
well organized state of, 130 .
Vital Fluid, see Solar fluid .

Voice of the Silence, 99 .
Volcanic eruptions produced by salamanders, 72 .
Vortices, whirling, of desire body, 131 .
War causes infant mortality, 177 , 179 .
Wave of spirituality inspired great religions, 7 .
Whipping children, evil of, 198 .
Will, lack of, racial defect, 198 .
Wind, changes of, caused by sylphs, 71 .
Word, Creative Fiat, 109 .
Word, creative, and key-note, 100 ;
God was, 106 ;
power of, 110 , 193 ;
still sounds in cosmos, 112 .
World, Desire, see Desire World .
World of Thought, see Thought, World of .
World, physical, world of form, 68 .
Worlds, higher, difficulty of investigating, 32 .
Yellow in stellar ray, life of Son, 124 ;
produces consciousness, 188 .
Zoroastrian religion, deities of, 86 .
[pg 227]

Advertisements

Rays From the Rose Cross
 The American Mystic Monthly
 A Monthly Magazine of Mystic Light devoted to philosophy, occultism, mystic masonry, astrology, and healing.
 Those who desire knowledge and guidance along the Path of the Western Wisdom Teachings will find this magazine a constant aid.
 It expounds and supports occult and mystical philosophy in a most instructive and interesting manner. It carries such special departments as:
Questions and Answers on Mystical Subjects
Editorial Discussion of Current Events
Astrological Readings
Occult Stories
One of the foremost magazines of its kind in America.
Price $2.00 per year in U. S. and Canada.
Other Countries, $2.25.
The Rosicrucian Fellowship,
Mt. Ecclesia
Oceanside, California.
[pg 228]
Rosicrucian Interpretation of Christianity
 ANCIENT TRUTHS IN MODERN DRESS
 Price 10c Each, Postfree
 No. 1. The Riddle of Life and Death.
 No. 2. Where Are the Dead?
 No. 3. Spiritual Sight and the Spiritual Worlds.
 No. 4. Sleep, Dreams, Trance, Hypnotism, Mediumship and Insanity.
 No. 5. Death and Life in Purgatory.
 No. 6. Life and Activity in Heaven.
 No. 7. Birth a Fourfold Event.
 No. 8. The Science of Nutrition, Health and Protracted Youth.
 No. 9. The Astronomical Allegories of the Bible.
 No. 10. Astrology; Its Scope and Limitations.
 No. 11. Spiritual Sight and Insight.
 No. 12. Parsifal.
 No. 13. The Angels as Factors in Evolution.
 No. 14. Lucifer, Tempter or Benefactor?
 No. 15. The Mystery of Golgotha and the Cleansing Blood.
 No. 16. The Star of Bethlehem; A Mystic Fact.
 No. 17. The Mystery of the Holy Grail.
 No. 18. The Lord's Prayer.
 No. 19. The Coming Force; Vril or What?
 No. 20. Fellowship and the Coming Race.
 These lectures are particularly suitable for beginners. Read consecutively, they give a comprehensive outline of our philosophy.
 THEY FIT THE POCKET
and allow a busy man to utilize time on cars en route to or from business.
 GIVE ONE TO A FRIEND
 It is an inexpensive and a helpful gift.
The Rosicrucian Fellowship,
Mt. Ecclesia
Oceanside, California.
[pg 229]
Correspondence Courses
 IN
 The Rosicrucian Philosophy and Astrology
 (1) Rosicrucian Philosophy :
 Using the Cosmo-Conception by Max Heindel as a textbook, this course of twelve lessons points to a logical explanation of the origin, evolution, and future development of mankind, and opens the way to a deeper knowledge of this great subject. This philosophy seeks to make Christianity a living factor in the world , and to combine the eternal facts of Science, Art, and Religion. This course is open to all those interested.
 (2) Astrology :
 We want to assist you in helping yourself and others. This correspondence course will teach you the importance of astrology as a phase of religion and a Divine Science. The one restriction is that our pupils may not prostitute the knowledge thus obtained for gain in any way. Anyone not engaged in fortune telling or similar methods of commercializing spiritual knowledge may be admitted to this course.
 For admission to these courses address,
 (I) Philosophy Secretary.
 (II) Astrology Secretary.
 The Rosicrucian Fellowship,
Mt. Ecclesia
Oceanside, California.
[pg 230]
THE
 Rosicrucian Cosmo-Conception
 By Max Heindel
 Eighth Edition With New 70 Page Index
 This book gives a complete outline of the Western Wisdom Teaching as far as it may be made public at the present time. The Rosicrucian Brotherhood from time to time gives out occult teachings to the public in such a manner

that their expression conforms to the intellectual development of the times. This is the latest of their communications.

Max Heindel was the accredited agent of the Rosicrucian Brotherhood, commissioned to give the contents of this book to the world. There is no other book that contains so complete an exposition of the factors that enter into the creation of the universe and of man and all its statements are in keeping with the results of scientific research.

Part I is a treatise on the Visible and the Invisible Worlds, Man and the Method of Evolution, Rebirth and the Law of Cause and Effect.

Part II takes up the scheme of Evolution in general and the Evolution of the Solar System and the Earth in particular.

Part III treats of Christ and His Mission, Future Development of Man and Initiation, Esoteric Training and a Safe Method of Acquiring First-hand Knowledge.

616 Pages. Cloth Bound. $2.00 Post-free.

The Rosicrucian Fellowship,
Mt. Ecclesia
Oceanside, California.

[pg 231]

The Message of the Stars

By Max Heindel and Augusta Foss Heindel

One of the most complete systems of character delineation and reading the horoscope for medical diagnosis yet given to modern astrology.

With many nontechnical articles to interest the general student of the occult, a simple method of

PROGRESSION AND PREDICTION,

and a new index for quickly locating desired information, it is indeed a classic in its realm.

In the section on Medical Astrology the authors have given a system that is based on years of practical experience. Thirty-six example horoscopes are included, and the subject is dealt with most thoroughly.

YOU NEED THIS BOOK!

708 Pages. Cloth Bound. $3.50 Postpaid.

The Rosicrucian Fellowship,
Mt. Ecclesia
Oceanside, California.

[pg 232]

The Web of Destiny

HOW MADE AND UNMADE

By Max Heindel

Including

The Occult Effect of Our Emotions

Prayer—A Magic Invocation

Practical Methods of Achieving Success

This book is based on personal occult investigations by the author, in which he uncovered many of the inner laws governing man's hidden springs of action.

It gives information regarding the Dweller on the Threshold, which every aspirant has to meet, usually at an early stage of his progress into the unseen worlds. It treats of the causes of obsession of men and animals. It describes how we create our environment and some of the causes of disease, pointing the way to final emancipation.

The part devoted to the emotions shows the function of desire, the color effects of emotion, and the results of worry and remorse.

Prayer is shown here as a magic invocation by which powerful forces may be marshalled. It throws much light on the nature of prayer, pointing out that true prayer is based on scientific principles which will bring results when rightly applied.

Written in a simple and narrative style, it offers at the same time serious instruction and pleasant relaxation.

175 Pages. Cloth Bound.

[pg 233]

Freemasonry and Catholicism

By Max Heindel

An Esoteric Treatise on the Underlying Facts regarding these two great Institutions as determined by occult investigation.

It explains in terms of Mystic Masonry the conflict between the Sons of Cain and the Sons of Seth, and unravels the allegory dealing with the building of Solomon's Temple, the Queen of Sheba, and the Grand Master, Hiram Abiff.

If you are interested in the symbols of Masonry, in knowing the source of these mysteries which have come down to us from past ages, this is the book you want.

Only a trained Seer could have read the Akashic Records of the past and given such a clear explanation of their meaning.

In addition, read what the author says about the famous Philosopher's Stone of the Alchemists, the Path of Initiation, and the Coming Age.

This Book Should Be in Every Mason's Library.

98 Pages. Cloth Bound. $1.00 Post-free.

The Rosicrucian Fellowship,
Mt. Ecclesia
Oceanside, California.

[pg 234]

Gleanings of a Mystic

By Max Heindel

This book is devoted to practical mysticism, bringing out a vast array of new information and fine points never before presented in this form. The information contained in this book will be of immense value to the student and aspirant, enabling them to make swifter progress in both their spiritual and material development.

A few chapter headings are appended to give a better idea of the contents:

Initiation—What It Is and Is Not.

The Sacraments of Communion, Baptism, and Marriage.

The Coming Christ.

The Coming Age.

Magic, White and Black.

Our Invisible Government.

Practical Precepts for Practical People.

Sound, Silence, and Soul Growth.

The Mysterium Magnum of the Rose Cross.

Stumbling Blocks.

Why I Am a Rosicrucian.

196 Pages. Cloth Bound. $2.00 Postpaid.

[pg 235]

The Rosicrucian Philosophy

IN QUESTIONS AND ANSWERS

By Max Heindel

A book of ready reference upon all

mystic matters, which ought to be in the library of every occult student. It comprises the answers to hundreds of questions asked of Max Heindel on the lecture platform.

PARTIAL LIST OF SUBJECTS:
Life after Death.
Life on Earth.
The Bible Teachings.
Spiritualistic Phenomena.
Clairvoyance.
Astrology.
Animals.

176 Pages. Cloth Bound. $2.00 Postpaid.

How Shall We Know Christ at His Coming?
By Max Heindel

This book tells us that Christ will return in an etheric, not a physical body. Hence mankind must develop the etheric body to the point where they can function in it consciously before Christ will return. Then they will possess the inner spiritual perception by which they will be able to recognize Him.

These matters are fully elucidated in this book.

29 Pages. Paper Bound. 15c Postfree.
The Rosicrucian Fellowship,
Mt. Ecclesia
Oceanside, California.

[pg 236]
In the Land of The Living Dead
AN OCCULT STORY
By Prentiss Tucker

Among the many post-war books, here is one to interest the soldier, student, and layman alike. Its appeal is general and lasting in that it portrays in story form the ever existing conditions on the superphysical planes. It inclines toward that thing called "The religion of the trenches," and will help to open the eyes of many a puzzled participant as well as of those who lost friends and relatives in the Great War.

Look at some of the chapter headings:
A Visit to the Invisible Planes.
A Sergeant's Experiences after "Passing out."
A Doughboy's Ideas on Religion.
Helping a Slain Soldier to Comfort His Mother.
A Crisis in Love.

168 Pages. Cloth Bound. $1.50 Postpaid.

[pg 237]
The Mystical Interpretation of Christmas
By Max Heindel

This treatise covers the Cosmic Significance of Christmas and the annual Sacrifice of Christ, traces the astrological interpretation up through the simplicity of nature worship, and sketches a glorious outlook for the coming age, which inspires the casual reader to seek more Light.

Here is a book most attractively bound in heavy mottled paper which, aside from its merit as a simple gift, is most useful in answering inquiries on the occult significance of its subject. The world is beginning to ask the greater meaning of this holy festival; it is well to be informed.

Heavy Paper Binding.
75 Cents Postpaid.

[pg 238]
Earthbound
By Augusta Foss Heindel

An addition to our Rosicrucian Christianity Series of twenty lectures. This pamphlet warns against the craze for phenomena, mediumship, and the ouija board. It cites concrete cases where those who held too closely to things of this earth were thereby held back in their progress after leaving the earthy body and passing onward to the unseen realms of being. It points out how this condition may be avoided; also how some prolong their stay in the Borderland close to the earth.

It describes the condition of those who are bound to the lower Desire World after death by sense affiliation, sorrow, or other causes, showing clearly their delusions and their activities.

13 pages. Paper Bound. Price 10c.

[pg 239]
Simplified Scientific Astrology
By Max Heindel
Fifth Edition.
With Max Heindel's Portrait

198 Pages. Cloth Bound. $1.50 Postpaid.

A complete textbook on the art of erecting a horoscope, making the process simple and easy for beginners. It also includes a

Philosophic Encyclopedia
—and—
Tables of Planetary Hours

The Philosophic Encyclopedia fills a long felt want both of beginners and advanced students for information concerning the underlying reasons for astrological dicta. It is a mine of knowledge arranged in such a manner as to be instantly accessible.

The Tables of Planetary Hours enable one to select the most favorable time for beginning new enterprises.

The unparalleled merits of this book have been amply attested by many thousands of enthusiastic students who have bought the first four editions.

No astrological student can afford to be without it.

[pg 240]
Mysteries of the Great Operas
By Max Heindel

Faust, Parsifal, The Ring of the Niebelung, Tannhauser, Lohengrin

Folk Lore and its interpretation through music has much to offer to the general reader as well as to the musician and occultist. These Myths conceal many of the hidden truths which are now being translated from symbol and allegory, and this attractive book is the key to these poetic tales of evolution, sacrifice, and unfoldment.

176 Pages. Cloth Bound. $2.00 Postpaid.

***